THE
PLACE OF
HELP

Discovery House

P U B L I S H E R S
BOX 3566 · GRAND RAPIDS. MI 49501

*PUBLISHING BOOKS THAT FEED
THE SOUL WITH THE WORD OF GOD.*

CHRISTIAN LITERATURE CRUSADE
Fort Washington, Pennsylvania 19034

THE PLACE OF HELP

God's Provision for our Daily Needs

OSWALD CHAMBERS

*Published through special arrangement with the
Oswald Chambers Publications Association Ltd.*

CONTENTS

	Publisher's Foreword	7
	Foreword	9
1.	The Place of Help	11
2.	The Way	17
3.	Two Sides to Fellowship	20
4.	Dissipated Devotion	24
5.	Skillful Soul-winning	30
6.	Love—Human and Divine	34
7.	The Passion for Christ	39
8.	Partakers of His Sufferings	43
9.	The Theology of Rest	48
10.	The Altar of Fellowship	51
11.	The Evening Test of Loyalty	55
12.	The Discipline of Disillusionment	59
13.	Did Jesus Christ Come for Peace?	66
14.	Spiritual Education	71
15.	The Makeup of a Worker	76
16.	Loyalty to the Forlorn Hope	80
17.	Spiritual Evolution	85
18.	At God's Discretion	89
19.	Celebration or Surrender?	93
20.	The Sacrament of Silence	98

21. Spiritual Confusion 102
22. The Long Trail to Spiritual Reality 106
23. Autobiography of Communion with God 110
24. Is He Your Master? 115
25. Why Are We Not Told Plainly? 120
26. The Transfigured Experience of Life 125
27. The Dawn That Transfigures Tears 129
28. The Sacrament of Sacrifice 134
29. Spiritual Discipleship 139
30. Sacramental Discipleship 143
31. The Limit of Dedication 148
32. The Spiritual "D.S.O." 152
33. Pain in the Dawn of Eternal Hope 158
34. The Honor of a Saint 165
35. Yearning to Recover God 174
36. Spiritual Inefficiency 178
37. With God at the Front 183
38. The Unspeakable Wonder 189
39. Acquaintance with Grief 194
40. Enthusiastic and Capable 202
41. The Throes of the Ultimate 205
42. Voice and Vision 213
43. The Plane of Spiritual Vigor 218
44. The Sense of Awe 222
45. Spiritual Malingering 227
46. The Deep Embarrassments of God 232
47. Getting into God's Stride 236
48. Disabling Shadows on the Soul 242

PUBLISHER'S FOREWORD

"Help" is the universal cry of the human heart. It describes the agony of the soul in need to which God lovingly responds in redemption. He answers as the person and place of help in Jesus Christ, providing help for the helpless and hope for the hopeless.

One of the excellencies of God is His being the *Place of Help*. Nothing and no one is so truly and so really the place and person from whom help comes as is He. Our need for help is *rescue* in the fullest sense and only He can provide it. He rescues us from our sin and ourselves, from our fallenness and our faults, from our helplessness and our hopelessness. *He is* the place of rescue.

It is Oswald Chambers method to focus on God and His provision for our need. That provision is Christ and only Christ. *He* is the person of help—we can find no other, there is no other, we need no other. "The way to the fulfillment of all life's highest ideals and deepest longings is the Lord Jesus Christ Himself."

The Publisher

FOREWORD

The honor of framing this brief foreword the writer owes to the fact of being one of the very few who heard all, or almost all, the addresses at the time they were given, and of having thus been able to sense the spirit of their setting.

In their selection no strict sequence as to dates has been observed, but they are roughly grouped as follows. The un- dated sermons were preached in England either to Sunday congregations in various places in country or in town (1908– 15), or at the Bible Training College, Clapham Common (1911–15); the dated ones belong to the period of Oswald Chambers's ministry under the Y.M.C.A. at Zeitoun, Egypt, a center to which men came from almost every unit of the Army in the Near East (1915–17).

The sermons entitled "Spiritual Discipleship" and "Sacra- mental Discipleship" were preached on the Sunday before Os- wald Chambers sailed for Egypt in October, 1915.

The talks at the B.T.C. were teaching talks. They lack of necessity the asides and illustrations that lit them up so de- lightfully, but it is easy in many cases to trace in the scriptural references the line of Bible study being pursued at the time each was delivered.

The sermons at Zeitoun in those years of strain and stress were the very sacrament of preaching: no one could doubt it who heard with the keen hearing of the spiritual ear the miracle of authentic stillness that falls upon an assembly of men in those rare moments when a man speaks to his hearers, spirit to spirit, and he and they alike know it. The moment passes, but the "inward and spiritual grace" abides—a sacramental permanent possession.

To all who knew Oswald Chambers, his life was the interpretation of his teaching; to those to whom it comes now in another form the meaning opens in the hidden individual ways of God. The writer believes that the Spirit of God is using this teaching in many lands to very many lives as a corrective to the wave of shallow thinking, and of shallower religious values that has swept across a section of the Christian communities everywhere.

By Oswald Chambers, men's minds are thrown back upon the deep fundamental things that govern human life in its threefold aspect of spirit, soul, and body: divine redemption is brought down to the very shores of our daily living: the cross of Calvary is shown to men as being the very heart and center of the revelation of God in the person of our Lord and Savior Jesus Christ.

Now "Unto Him that loved us, . . . to Him be glory and dominion for ever and ever." Amen.

One of the B.T.C. Students
28 September 1935

THE PLACE OF HELP

"I will lift up my eyes to the hills—from whence comes my help? My help comes from the LORD, who made heaven and earth" (Ps. 121:1–2).

This rendering puts it in the form of a question. "I will lift up my eyes to the hills—from whence comes my help?" and recalls Jeremiah's statement: "In vain is help looked to from the mountains." I want to apply that statement spiritually.

Great Aspirations

Mountains stir intense hope and awaken vigor, but ultimately leave the climber exhausted and spent. Great men and great saints stir in us great aspirations and a great hopefulness, but leave us ultimately exhausted with a feeling of hopelessness; the inference we draw is that these people were built like that, and all that is left for us to do is to admire. Longfellow says: "Lives of great men all remind us we can make our lives sublime," but I question whether this is profoundly true. The lives of great men leave us with a sense of our own littleness which paralyzes us in our effort to be anything else. Going back to the setting of this psalm, one realizes that the exquisite beauty of the mountain scenery awakens lofty aspirations; the limitless spaces above the highest mountain-peak, the snow-clad summit, and the scarred side ending in foliage and beauty as it sweeps to the valley below, stand as a symbol for all that is high and lofty and aspiring. When one is young this is the type of scenery most reveled in, the blood runs quicker, the air is purer and more vigorous, and things seem possible to the out-look that were not possible when we lived in the valleys; but as one gets older, and realizes the limitation not only of physi-cal life but in the inner life, the remembrance of the mountains and of mountain-top experiences leaves us a little wistful with an element of sadness, an element perhaps best expressed by the phrase, "What might have been, had we always been true to the truth, had we never sinned, had we never made mis-takes!" Even such simple considerations as these bring us to the heart of the psalmist's song in this pilgrim song book—"I will lift up my eyes to the hills—from whence comes my help?" And the psalmist answers, "My help comes from the LORD, who made heaven and earth,"—and there we have the essence of the spiritual truth. Not to the great things God has done, not to the noble saints and noble lives He has made, but to God Himself does the psalmist point.

The study of biography is always inspiring, but it has this one drawback, that it is apt to leave the life more given to sentiment and thinking and perhaps less to endeavor than is usually supposed; but when we realize what the psalmist is pointing out and what the New Testament so strongly insists on, that is, "My help comes from the LORD," we are able to understand such a mountain-peak character as the apostle Paul saying "Follow my ways which be in Christ." We have not been told to follow in all the footsteps of the mountain-like characters, but in the footsteps of their faith, because their faith is in a person.

Great Attainments

This is such an important theme that it will profit us to look at it from another aspect. This is the age when education is placed on the very highest pinnacle. In every civilized country we are told that if we will educate the people and give them better surroundings, we shall produce better characters. Such talk and such theories stir aspirations, but they do not work out well in reality. The kingdom within must be adjusted first before education can have its true use. To educate an unregenerate man is but to increase the possibility of cultured degradation. No one would wish to belittle the lofty attainments of education and culture, but we must realize we have to put them in their high, mighty, second place. Their relationship in human life is second, not first. The man whom God made is first, and the God who made him is his only help. God seems to point this out all through His book-Moses, learned in all the learning of the Egyptian schools, the highest and ablest prophet-statesman conceivable, realizes with a keenness and poignancy the bondage and degradation of his brethren, and sees that he is the one to deliver them: but God sends him for forty years into a wilderness to feed sheep. He removes first of all the big "I am" and then the little "I am" out of him. Read the account carefully; you will find that at the end of those forty years, when God spoke to Moses again, saying, "Come now, therefore, and I will send you to Pharaoh, that you may bring My people, the children of Israel, out of Egypt," Moses said "Who am I?" All this points out one thing, that the ability of a man to help his fellow man lies lastingly with God and is not concerned with his aspirations or his education or his attainments.

The same thing emerges in chapter 15 of John's gospel where our Lord instructs His disciples about the new dispensation "I am." "I am the Vine . . . ." If the dominant identity of the disciple is not built up by God Himself, in vain are the mountains looked to for help. There may be some who are trying by aspiration and prayer and consecration and obe- dience, built up from looking at the lives that stand like moun- tain peaks, to attain a like similarity of character, and they are woefully lagging behind; their lips, as it were, have grown pale in the intense struggle, and they falter by the way, and the characters that used to stir intense hopefulness leave the soul sighing over "what might have been," but now can never be. To such a reader let the message of Psalm 121 come with new hope, "My help comes from the LORD, who made heaven and earth." A strong saintly character is not the production of human breeding or culture, it is the manufacture of God.

Great Admirations

Take it from another aspect. There are people today who are exalting our Lord as a teacher, saying, in effect, that they believe in the Sermon on the Mount and its high ideals but not in the cross; that all that is necessary is to place the pure noble ideals of the Sermon on the Mount before mankind and let men strive to attain; that there is no need for a sacrificial death. When minds and men and countries are very young in thinking, this sort of statement and teaching has a wonderful fascination, but we sooner or later learn that if Jesus Christ was merely a teacher, He adds to the burdens of human nature, for He erects an ideal that human nature can never attain. He tantalizes us by statements that poor human nature can never fit itself for. By no prayer, by no self-sacrifice, by no devotion, and by no climbing can any man attain to that "Blessed are the pure in heart," which Jesus Christ says is essential to seeing God.

When we come to the New Testament interpretation of our Lord we find He is not a teacher, we find He is a Savior. We find that His teaching is but a statement of the kind of life we will live when we have let Him remake us by means of His cross and by the incoming of His Spirit. The life of Jesus is to be made ours, not by our imitation, not by our climbing, but by means of His death. It is not admiration for holiness, nor aspirations after holiness, but *attainment* of holiness, and this is ours from God, not from any ritual of imitation.

I would like to commend this thought for the instruction and courage of those whose hearts are fainting in the way, from whom the ideals of youth have fled, to whom life holds out no more promises. For thirty years or more it may be that life has been a boundless romance of possibilities; beckoning signs from lofty mountain peaks have lured the spirit on; but now the burden and the heat of the day have come and the mountain tops are obscured in a dazing, dazzling heat, and the road is dusty and the mileage long, and the feet are weak and the endeavor is exhausted. Let me bring the message contained in this psalm, even as a cup of water from the clear sparkling spring of life. "My help comes from the LORD, Who made heaven and earth." He will take you up, He will remake you, He will make your soul young and will restore to you the years that the cankerworm has eaten, and place you higher than the loftiest mountain peak, safe in the arms of the Lord Himself, secure from all alarms, and with an imperturbable peace that the world cannot take away.

This psalm is one of the fifteen that the people sang and chanted on their ways of weary pilgrimage to the mighty concourse and festivity of God's hosts, and it is well called one of the "pilgrim psalms." The psalmist goes on to say, "The sun shall not strike you by day, nor the moon by night. The LORD shall preserve you from all evil," so that there be no fainting by the way. "The LORD shall preserve your going out and your coming in from this time forth, and even forevermore."

To whom are you looking? To some great mountain-like character? Are you even looking at the Lord Jesus Christ as a great mountain-like character? It is the wrong way; help does not come that way. Look to the Lord alone, and come with the old pauper cry

Just as I am, without one plea
But that Thy blood was shed for me,
And that Thou bid'st me come to Thee—
O Lamb of God, I come.

Any soul, no matter what his experience, that gets beyond this attitude is in danger of "falling from grace". Oh, the security, the ineffable rest of knowing that the God who made the mountains can come to our help! Let us hasten at once under the "shadow of the Almighty," to the "secret place of the Most High," for *there* shall no evil befall us. Jesus said, "the one who comes to Me I will by no means cast out."

THE WAY

The Waylessness

To the prophets and poets of the Bible, life is a wayless wilderness. In it there are many voices crying, "This is the way," many ideals with signposts claiming to point out the way. It would be interesting to trace the sadness that lays hold of the minds of those who have never known the one and true living way, in whose outlook the waylessness of life seems to be the dominant note. Take, for instance, Thomas Carlyle; his mighty literary genius and his instinct for God made him ask in an insurgent manner why God kept silence, why He did not manifest Himself amid all the corruption and shams of life. No wonder his mind deepened into a dark stoicism, since he never saw that God had manifested Himself in that He had pointed the way out of all the mysteries of life in the cross of our Lord Jesus Christ. Or take our poets, those who have never known the way—their "sweetest songs are those that tell of saddest thought." The feeling of uncertainty as to the issue, and the strange vagueness of the way is the inspiration of their thought. Or take our own personal moods when we are roused out of our commonplace equilibrium and the sense grows upon us strongly of the implicit kinship of the human spirit with the untrodden waylessness of life—until a man finds the Lord Jesus Christ, his heart and brain and spirit will lead him astray.

The Wayfarers

There are many ways in which a man's life may be suddenly struck by an immortal moment, when the true issues of his life, "the spirit's true endowments, stand out plainly from its false ones," and he knows in that moment whether he is "pursuing or the right way or the wrong way, to its triumph or undoing." Such a moment may come by conviction of sin, or it may come through the opening up of the vast isolation of a man's own nature which makes him afraid. Or it may come with the feeling that somewhere he will meet One who will put him on the way to solve his implicit questions, one who will satisfy the last aching abyss of the human heart, and put within his hands the key to unlock the secret treasures of life. There are many gates into the holy city, and many avenues by which God may enter the human soul.

To all whose souls have been awakened by these moods or by conviction of sin, for whom life has been profoundly altered so that it can never be the same again—to all such the voice of the Lord Jesus Christ comes as the voice of the eternal: "I am the way." If a man will resign himself in implicit trust to the Lord Jesus, he will find that He leads the wayfaring soul into the green pastures and beside the still waters, so that even when he goes through the dark valley of the shadow of some staggering episode, he will fear no evil. Nothing in life or death, time or eternity, can stagger that soul from the certainty of the way for one moment.

The Wayfinder

The way is missed by everyone who has not the childlike heart; we have to go humbly lest we miss the way of life just because it is so simple. God has hidden these things from the wise and prudent and revealed them unto babes. When a man has been found by the Lord Jesus and has given himself to Him in unconditional surrender, the fact that he has found the way is not so much a conscious possession as an unconscious inheritance. Explicit certainty is apt to make a man proud, and that spirit can never be in the saint. The life of the saint who has discovered the way is the life of a little child; he discerns the will of God implicitly.

One of the significant things about those who are in the way is that they have a strong family likeness to Jesus, His peace marks them in an altogether conspicuous manner. The light of the morning is on their faces, and the joy of the endless life is in their hearts. Wherever they go, men are gladdened or healed, or made conscious of a need.

The way to the fulfillment of all life's highest ideals and its deepest longings is the Lord Jesus Christ Himself. How patiently He waits until, having battered ourselves against the impregnable bars of our universe, we turn at last, humbled and bruised, to His arms, and find that all our fightings and fears, all our willfulness and waywardness, were unnecessary had we but been simple enough to come to Him at the first. "There is a way that seems right to a man, but its end is the way of death." God grant that for our own sakes, for the sake of those near and dear to us, for the sake of the wide world, and for the sake of the Lord Jesus Christ, we may come to this new and living way, where "whoever walks the road . . . shall not go astray . . . but the redeemed shall walk there . . . with singing, with everlasting joy on their heads."

TWO SIDES TO FELLOWSHIP

"Whatever I tell you in the dark, speak in the light; and what you hear in the ear, preach on the housetops" (Matt. 10:27).

"Whatever I tell you in the dark . . . ."
Let it be understood that the darkness our Lord speaks of is not darkness caused by sin or disobedience, but rather darkness caused from excess of light. There are times in the life of every disciple when things are not clear or easy, when it is not possible to know what to do or say. Such times of darkness come as a discipline to the character and as the means of fuller knowledge of the Lord. Such darkness is a time for listening, not for speaking. This aspect of darkness as a necessary side to fellowship with God is not unusual in the Bible (see Isa. 5:30; 50:10; 1 Pet. 1:6–7). The Lord shares the darkness with His disciple: "Whatever I tell you in the dark . . . ." He is there. He knows all about it. The sense of mystery must always be, for mystery means being guided by obedience to someone who knows more than I do. On the Mount of Transfiguration this darkness from excess of light is brought out. "They were fearful as they entered the cloud," but in the cloud "they saw no one anymore, but only Jesus with themselves."

In this side of fellowship with God the disciple must not mourn or fret for the light, nor must he put forth self-effort or any determination of the flesh or kindle a fire of his own. Many tendencies which lead to delusion arise just here. When the disciple says in his heart "there must be a break; God must reveal Himself," he loses sight altogether that in the darkness God wants him to listen and not fuss. "In quietness and confidence shall be your strength."

A disciple must be careful not to talk in the darkness; the listening ear is to be his characteristic, not listening to the voice of sympathizing fellow disciples, or to the voice of self-pity, but listening only to the voice of the Lord, "Whatever I tell you in the dark, speak in the light; and what you hear in the ear, preach on the housetops." Not what the disciple says in public prayer, not what he preaches from pulpit or platform, not what he writes on paper or in letters, but what he is in his heart which God alone knows, determines God's revelation of Himself to him. Character determines revelation (see Ps. 18:24–26). "With the merciful You will show Yourself merciful" (v. 25). "Say to them, 'As I live,' says the LORD, 'just as you have spoken in My hearing, so I will do to you'" (Num. 14:28).

There is another side to fellowship: "Whatever I tell you in the dark, speak in the light." What are we speaking in the light? Many talk glibly and easily about stupendous truths which they believe, but the Lord has never revealed them to them in darkness. God's providential leadings will take the one who proclaims those glorious truths into tribulation and darkness whereby they can be made part of his own possession. Jesus tells us what we are to speak in the light: "Whatever I tell you in the dark."

All servants and handmaidens of the Lord have to partake in this discipline of darkness, to have the ear trained to listen to their master's words. Our Lord never gives private illuminations to special favorites. His way is ever twofold: the development of character, and the descent of divine illumination through the Word of God. Many are talking in the light today, and many voices have gone forth, but Jesus says, "My sheep hear My voice . . . they will by no means follow a stranger, but will flee from him, for they do not know the voice of strangers." At the beginning of a disciplining spell of providential darkness, the tumult and the noise may hinder the spirit from hearing the voice of the Lord, but sooner or later the disciple, at first inclined to say it thundered and to be afraid, says, "Thy voice is on the rolling air; I see Thee in the setting sun, and in the rising, Thou art fair."

The voice of the Lord listened to in darkness is so entrancing that the finest of earth's voices are never afterwards mistaken for the voice of the Lord. Where are those in this fellowship of the Lord found today? "If we walk in the light as He is in the light, we have fellowship with one another." The fellowship of the disciples is based not on natural affinities of taste but on fellowship in the Holy Spirit, a fellowship that is constrained and enthralled by the love and communion of our Lord and Savior Jesus Christ. When both sides of this fellowship, listening in darkness and speaking in light, are realized, no darkness can terrify anymore.

Thou hast done well to kneel and say,
"Since He Who gave can take away,
And bid me suffer, I obey!"
And also well to tell my heart
Thy good lies in the bitterest part,
And thou wilt profit by her smart . . .
Nor with thy share of work be vexed;
Though incomplete and e'en perplexed,
It fits exactly to the next.
What seems too dark to thy dim sight
May be a shadow, seen aright,

Making some brightness doubly bright—
The flash that struck thy tree—no more
To shelter thee—lets Heaven's blue floor
Shine where it never shone before.

Oh, the unspeakable benediction of the "treasures of darkness!" But for the night in the natural world we should know nothing of moon or stars, or of all the incommunicable thoughtfulness of the midnight. So spiritually it is not the days of sunshine and splendor and liberty and light that leave their lasting and indelible effect upon the soul but those nights of the spirit in which, shadowed by God's hand, hidden in the dark cleft of some rock in a weary land, He lets the splendors of the outskirts of Himself pass before our gaze. It is such moments as these that insulate the soul from all worldliness and keep it in an "other-worldliness" while carrying on work for the Lord and communion with Him in this present evil world.

"The darkness shall not hide from You, but the night shines as the day; the darkness and the light are both alike to You."

DISSIPATED DEVOTION

"Take heed to yourself that you do not offer your burnt offerings in every place that you see; but in the place which the LORD chooses, in one of your tribes, there you shall offer your burnt offerings, and there you shall do all that I command you" (Deut. 12:13–14).

An unusual theme, but this Old Testament ritual which refers to the people of God having too many shrines, has a lesson of penetrating importance for us in the New Testament dispensation, which is that there is a willful element in our consecration that must be exterminated.

The impulse of worship is natural in the majority of human beings, and we must make the distinction very clear between the impulse of worship in an unregenerate spirit and the impulse of worship in a saint. Natural devotion chooses its own altars, its own setting, the scene of its own martyrdom. It would be very entrancing if a human being could go to martyrdom in such moods, having arranged the spectators and the scenery to suit his own ambition; but this Old Testament passage says that God chooses the place for the offering. This aims at the very root of the whole matter. We do not consecrate our gifts to God, they are not ours to give; we consecrate ourselves to God, that is, we give up the right to ourselves to Him.

Place of Consecration

A remarkable thing is that the place of the altar is not mentioned because evidently it was continually being changed. If it had been always at one place, the people would have become devoted to that place and would have made it a scene of religious festival without any indication of real devotion to God.

All through the prophets one hears the continual cry that the people have fasted or feasted for their own pleasure, they have been religious because it suited them; but the only devotion which is acceptable to God is the devotion on the part of a regenerate soul that starts from a full-hearted consecration, which by binding the sacrifice of itself to the altar of God, receives from God the supreme sanctification which identifies it for ever with the life of the Lord. The place of this devotion can never be discovered by human intelligence, or natural spirituality, but only by the Spirit of God.

It must be borne in mind that the burnt offering is not the sin offering. The apostle Paul shows us distinctly the place of the altar, and the sacrifice God wants, "I beseech you therefore, brethren, by the mercies of God, that you present your bodies a living sacrifice . . . .", literally, give up your right to yourself. That people find it extremely difficult to get to this place is true, and the reason is not difficult to find. We choose our own altars, and say, "Yes, we will devote ourselves to the foreign field," or "we will give ourselves to slum work," "to work in some orphanage," or to "rescue work." All this commends itself thoroughly to the natural heart of a man, but it is not the place the Lord chooses.

That place is discernible only by the Holy Spirit, and the offering is prompted not by devotion to duty, or devotion to a doctrine, but by devotion to a divine being. When our Lord talked to the woman of Samaria He pointed out that both Jews and Samaritans had begun to worship a place instead of God, but He said, "the hour is coming, and now is, when the true worshipers will worship the Father in spirit and truth."

Purpose of Consecration

In the general aspect of consecration one is easily misled by those who are possessed of natural piety. People talk about seeing God in nature, and are in danger of mistaking the impulse that seeks after God for God Himself. Paul makes that distinction very clear in Acts 17:27, "so that they should seek the Lord, in the hope that they might grope for Him and find Him, though He is not far from each one of us." The natural heart of man interprets that to mean that the instinct to worship, and to make an altar of devotion where he chooses, is the very instinct of God, whereas Paul implies that it is instinct feeling after God.

The altar of God's choosing is not approached by feelings of devotion or emotions of worship; that is why it is difficult to discover it. All natural religion reaches its climax in ritual, in the beauties of aesthetic and sensuous worship. God's altar is discerned only by the Holy Spirit when that Spirit is in a man.

The dissipation of devotion is seen over and over again in the practical issues of our lives. People give their lives to many things they have no business to. No one has any right to give up the right to himself or to herself to anyone but God Almighty, and devotion to a cause, no matter how noble or how beautiful, nowhere touches the profundity of this lesson. When we are told we must give up our right to ourselves to Jesus Christ, we are bound to ask—if we do not ask, we have not grasped the situation thoroughly "Who is it that asks this tremendous devotion? Is there any principle, any cause, any enterprise on the face of the earth of such importance that a man has to give the very highest he has, namely, his right to himself, for it?" The only being who dare ask of me this supreme sacrifice is the Lord Jesus Christ.

Satan's great aim is to deflect us from the center. He will allow us to be devoted "to death" to any cause, any enterprise, to anything but the Lord Jesus. Is anyone roused by the Spirit of God to wonder whether the object to which he is devoting his life has been chosen in a selfish consecration or not? It is so easy for a young convert, after listening to a missionary, to say God has given him a call *there*, and deliberately to choose to consecrate his life to that place. And that sort of thing is commended all over the Christian world, but I question whether it is commended by God. The tremendous worldwide instinct is of God. No soul has ever been saved or sanctified who did not instantly lose sight of country and of kindred, in the determination to do God's will; but immediately the desire and ambition of the individual chooses the altar, the scene of sacrifice, his devotion is dissipated.

Whenever our Lord talked about discipleship He brought out that fundamental thought "If anyone desires to come after Me, let him . . . take up his cross daily, and follow Me." Jesus Christ distinctly stated that He came to do the will of His Father. "I must work the works of Him who sent Me." His first obedience was not to the needs of men, but to the will of God. He nowhere chose the altar of His sacrifice, God chose it for Him. He chose to make His life a willing and obedient sacrifice that His Father's purpose might be fulfilled, and He says, "As the Father has sent Me, I also send you."

Position of Consecration

Are we putting the needs of mankind, heathen or otherwise, as the ground of our consecration? The amount of mistaken zeal and energy and passion and martyrdom thrown into

work for God, that has to come under the category of dissipated devotion, because people have chosen the scene of their
own worship, is appalling. God grant that we may accept the
primary call of the saint, which is to do the will of his Lord,
and the one vivid experience in the heart is personal, passionate devotion to Jesus Christ.

Paul actually says, "Though I give my body to be burned,
but have not love, it profits me nothing." This is the place in
which nine out of every ten of us are deluded. Because men
and women devote themselves to martyrdom for a cause, they
think they have struck the profoundest secret of religion;
whereas they have but exhibited the heroic spirit that is in all
human beings, and have not begun to touch the great fundamental secret of spiritual Christianity, which is wholehearted,
absolute consecration of myself to Jesus, not to His cause, not
to His "league of pity," but to Himself personally. "For we do
not preach ourselves, but Christ Jesus the Lord, and ourselves
your servants for Jesus' sake," as Paul says in 2 Corinthians
4:5. We are the servants of men, says Paul, not primarily
because their needs have arrested us, but because Jesus Christ
is our Lord; not because we feel the clamant needs of our age or
any such sounding timbrel, but that the Lord Jesus Christ has
saved and sanctified us and now He is Lord of our lives and
makes us unconsciously the servants of other men, not for their
sakes but for His own. This is the secret of presenting the
burnt offering on the altar that God chooses.

Passion of Consecration

When the "passion for souls" has not this center it is a
dangerous passion. The socialist has a passion for souls, but the
saint's passion for souls is not for man's sake primarily, but for
the sake of the Lord Jesus Christ. This is the source of all
evangelical missionary enterprise. The appeal is not to be put

on the ground that the heathen are perishing without the knowledge of God; that appeal awakens a willful devotion which dissipates the energies of the life. But let the preacher take back his hearer and his would-be devotee to the Garden of Gethsemane, to the still midnight in the quiet wood, to the pale moon's passionless gleam on each tree, and then in imagination again picture all prostrate on the ground, our King, Redeemer, God, whose bloody sweat, like heavy dew, stains the sod, and let the Holy Spirit ring through the preacher's and the hearer's heart, "This is the cost of having loved you."

And let him take the hearer and his own heart back to Calvary, to that "historic pole" of time and eternity, the cross of Christ, and then let the passion and power of the Holy Spirit so seize hold of heart and brain and imagination that the sacrifice is bound with cords unto the horns of the altar and the life is entirely at the disposal of God.

It is one thing to behold the haggard, starved, sin-stained, brokenhearted faces of men, but that is not sufficient for Christian enterprise. At the back of these faces must ever be seen the "Face marred more than any man's," until the passion of the whole world's anguish that forced its way through His heart, may force its way through our hearts too, until we are His forever, having drunk the cup of communion with His cross that shall identify us body, soul, and spirit as Christ's.

SKILLFUL SOUL-WINNING

"He must increase, but I must decrease" (John 3:30).

Decreasing into His Purpose

The most delicate mission on earth is to win souls for Jesus without deranging their affections and affinities and sympathies by our own personal fascination. There is neither discouragement nor pensive humility in John's statement, but the passionate realization of his position. As Christian workers we are about the most sacred business, seeking to win souls to the Lord Jesus, ministering to the holy relationship of bridegroom and bride. That is our business, and we must be watchful lest any mood or disposition of our own should give a false impression of the bridegroom and scare away the prospective bride. We are here for His sake, and we have to take care lest we damage His reputation. It may sometimes mean scaring a soul away from ourselves in order that Jesus Christ's attraction may tell.

Be jealously careful lest the impression given of our Lord in a public address is effaced when we come into the homes of the hearers. A beautiful saint may be a hindrance because he does not present Jesus Christ, but only what He has done, and the impression is left "What a fine character!" The *worker* is increasing all the time, not Jesus Christ.

Decoying into His Power

Spiritual moods are as sensitive and delicate as the awakenings of early love; the most exquisite thing in the human soul is that early mood of the soul when it first falls in love with the Lord. By Christian courtesy to Jesus Christ, we should confirm the desire and love which has been awakened in souls wooed by our messages until we see them partners of Him who is the chiefest among ten thousand, the altogether lovely one. It means no rest in intercession until the soul has long lost sight of the worker; he needs him no more because he has got the Lord. We are apt to interfere in lives and produce fanatics instead of men and women devoted to Jesus because we have not been friends of the bridegroom. We decoy them into our sect or our personal point of view instead of into His power. John's joy is this—At last they are to see the bridegroom! "He must increase, but I must decrease!" It is said not in sadness but in joy.

The watcher of souls for God has to get them not so much out of sin and wrong as to see Jesus. If you become a necessity to a soul you have got out of God's order, your great need as a worker is to be a friend of the bridegroom. Your goodness and purity ought never to attract attention to itself, it ought simply to be a magnet to draw others to Jesus; if it does not draw them to Him it is not holiness of the right order, it is an influence which will awaken inordinate affection and lead souls off into side issues. Over and over again we come in and prevent and say, "This, or that, must not be," and instead of being friends of the bridegroom we are sympathizing snares, and the soul is not able to say, "He or she was a friend of the bridegroom," but, "He or she was a thief and stole my affections away from Jesus Christ and located them elsewhere, and so I lost the vision."

Delighting in His Provision

When once you see a soul in sight of the claims of Jesus, you know your influence has been in the right direction, and instead of putting out a hand to withhold the throes, pray that they grow ten times stronger until no power on earth or in hell can ever hold that soul from Jesus Christ (cf. Luke 14:26). Beware of rejoicing in the wrong thing with a soul, but see that you rejoice at the right thing. "The friend of the bride-groom, who stands and hears him, rejoices greatly because of the bridegroom's voice. Therefore this joy of mine is fulfilled."

It is not sin that hinders, but our not living as friends of the bridegroom. Suppose you talk about depending on God and how wonderful it is, and then others see that in your own immediate concerns you do not depend on Him a bit, but on your own wits. It makes them say, "Well, after all, it's a big pretense, there is no almighty Christ to depend on anywhere, it is all mere sentiment." The impression left is that Jesus Christ is not real to you. "John performed no sign, but all the things that John spoke about this Man were true" (John 10:41).

Devoted to Him Personally

In order to maintain friendship and loyalty to Christ, be much more careful of your moral and vital relationship to Him than any other thing, even obedience. Sometimes there is noth-ing to obey, the only thing to do is to maintain your vital connection with Jesus Christ, to see that nothing interferes with your relationship to Him. Only at occasional times do we have to obey; when a crisis arises we have to find out what God's will is, but the greater part of our life is not conscious obedience, but this maintained relationship. To have our eyes on successful service is one of the greatest snares to a Christian worker, for it has in it the peril of evading the soul's concentration on Jesus Christ, and instead of being friends of the bridegroom we become antichrists in our domain, working against Him while we use His weapons; amateur providences with the jargon of divine providence, and when the bridegroom does speak we shall not hear His voice. Decreasing to the absolute effacing of the worker, till he or she is never thought of again, is the true result of devotion, and John says, "That is my joy. Watch until you hear the bridegroom's voice in the life of a soul, never mind what havoc, what upset it brings, what crumblings of health. Rejoice with divine hilarity over that soul because the bridegroom's voice has been heard."

LOVE—HUMAN AND DIVINE

"Love never fails" (1 Cor. 13:8).

"Love never fails!" What a wonderful phrase that is! but what a still more wonderful thing the reality of that love must be; greater than prophecy—that vast forthtelling of the mind and purpose of God; greater than the practical faith that can remove mountains; greater than philanthropic self-sacrifice; greater than the extraordinary gifts of emotions and ecstasies and all eloquence; and it is *this* love that is shed abroad in our hearts by the Holy Spirit which is given unto us.

The Highest Human Love

"Greater love has no one than this, than to lay down one's life for his friends" (John 15:13).

This wonderful verse, quoted so often during this terrible war, has suffered from contortions of belittling as well as of exaggeration; but the great words stand as those of the Lord Jesus Christ. They exhibit the highest human love, not the highest divine love. The love that lays down the life for a man's friends is irrespective of religious faith or of lack of it. Atheists and pagans, saints and sinners alike, have exhibited this highest human love.

The revival of this greatest human love has been superb during this war, but there has not been as yet any sign of a corresponding great revival of self-sacrificing love on the part of the church of Christ. Self-regarding love is part weakness, part selfishness, and part romance; and it is this self-regarding love that so counterfeits the higher love that, to the majority, love is too often looked upon as a weak sentimental thing.

"My Utmost for the Highest" was the motto of the great artist G. F. Watts, and it has very evidently been the watchword of thousands of young men whose names only figure now on the list of the killed. But let it never be forgotten that the highest human love has nothing to do with religious faith, and the distortion of this mighty statement of Christ Jesus arises from the misunderstanding of this point.

Probably the finest scriptural incident illustrating the highest human love is recorded in 2 Samuel 23:15–17.

The Highest Divine Love

"But God demonstrates His own love toward us, in that while we were still sinners, Christ died for us" (Rom. 5:8).

This is the characteristic of the divine love: not that God lays down His life for His friends, but that He lays down His life for His enemies (v. 10). That is not human love. It does not mean that no human being has ever laid down his life for his enemies, but it does mean that no human being ever did so without having received the divine nature through the redemption of our Lord.

This statement is alien to many modern minds imbued with evolutionary conceptions, because that type of intellectual thinking dislikes any break between the human and the divine; it is easy to say that human love and divine love are one and the same thing; actually they are very far from being the same. It is also easy to say that human virtues and God's nature are one and the same thing; but this, too, is actually far from the truth. We must square our thinking with facts. Sin has come in and made a hiatus between human and divine love, between human virtues and God's nature, and what we see now in human nature is only the remnant and refraction of the divine. Our Lord clearly indicates that a man needs to be born from above before he can possess or exhibit the oneness of the human and divine in his own person. In theoretic conception the human and the divine are one; in actual human life sin has made them two. Jesus Christ makes them one again by the efficacy of the atonement. Hence the distinction is not merely theological, but experiential.

"God demonstrates His own love." Human relationships may be used to illustrate God's love, for example, the love of father, mother, wife, lover; but illustration is not identity. Human love may illustrate the divine, it is not identical with the divine love because of sin. God's own love is so strange to our natural conceptions that we see no love in it; not until we are awakened by the conviction of our sin and anarchy do we realize God's great love towards us "while we were still sinners."

Tennyson's phrase, "We needs must love the highest when we see it, not Lancelot, nor another," is sufficiently true to be dangerously wrong; for when the religious people of our Lord's day saw the highest incarnate before them, they hated Him and crucified Him.

The words of the prophet Isaiah are humiliatingly true of us. When we see the highest, He is to us as "a root out of dry ground. He has no form or comeliness; and when we see Him, there is no beauty that we should desire Him" (Isa. 53:2). The highest divine love is not only exhibited in the extreme amazement of the tragedy of Calvary, but in the laying down of the divine life through the thirty years of Nazareth, through the three years of popularity, scandal, and hatred, and furthermore in the long pre-incarnate years (cf. Rev. 13:8).

The cross is the supreme moment in time and eternity, and it is the concentrated essence of the very nature of the divine love. God lays down His life in the very creation we utilize for our own selfish ends. God lays down His life in His long-suffering patience with the civilized worlds which men have erected on God's earth in defiance of all He has revealed. The self-expenditure of God for His enemies in the life and death of our Lord Jesus Christ becomes the great bridge over the gulf of sin whereby human love may cross over and be embraced by the divine love, the love that never fails.

The Highest Christian Love

"No longer do I call you servants; . . . but I have called you friends" (John 15:15).

This is the wonderful way in which our Lord connects the highest human love with the highest divine love; the connection is in His disciples. The emphasis is on the deliberate laying down of the life, not in one tragic crisis, but in the gray face of actual facts unillumined by romance, obscured by the mist of the utter commonplace, spending the life out deliberately day by day for my divine Lord and His friends—this is the love that never fails; and remember, the love that never fails is not human love alone, nor divine love alone, but the at-one-ment of them in the disciples of Jesus.

We reveal the impoverished meanness of our conceptions by the words we use in the actual business of life—"economy," "insurance," "diplomacy." These words cover by euphemism our ghastly disbelief in our heavenly Father. "Therefore you shall be perfect, just as your Father in heaven is perfect," and the connection of this perfection with its context must be observed. Its context is Matthew 5:45, "that you may be sons of your Father in heaven; for He makes His sun rise on the evil and on the good, and sends rain on the just and on the unjust." Our Lord means by being perfect then obviously that we exhibit in our actual relationships to men as they are, the hospitality and generosity our heavenly Father has exhibited to us. In 2 Corinthians 4:7–11, Paul makes it plain that there are no ideal conditions of life, but "My Utmost for His Highest" has to be carried out in the actual conditions of human life.

The highest Christian love is not devotion to a work or to a cause, but to Jesus Christ. In the early days of our Lord's life the grief and astonishment of Mary and Joseph was caused by this very thing, "And He said to them, 'Why is it that you sought Me? Did you not know that I must be about My Father's business [in My Father's house]? But they did not understand the statement which He spoke to them" (Luke 2:49–50). Causes are good, and work is good, but love in these fails. The laying down of the life for Jesus Christ's sake exhibits the Christian love that never fails. Our Lord was viewed as wild and erratic because He did not identify Himself with the cause of the Pharisees or with the Zealots, yet He laid down His life as the servant of Jehovah. "Therefore Jesus also, that He might sanctify the people with His own blood, suffered outside the gate," and the writer immediately follows it up with the injunction, "Therefore let us go forth to Him, outside the camp, bearing His reproach. For here we have no continuing city, but we seek the one to come" (Heb. 13:12–14).

Thank God that we have the glorious fighting chance of identifying ourselves with our Lord's interests in other people in the love that never fails, for that love "suffers long and is kind; love does not envy; does not parade itself, is not puffed up; does not behave rudely, does not seek its own, is not provoked, thinks no evil; does not rejoice in iniquity, but rejoices in the truth; bears all things, believes all things, hopes all things, endures all things. Love never fails."

THE PASSION FOR CHRIST

"You shall be witnesses to Me" (Acts 1:8).

These words of our risen Lord were spoken just before His ascension. We have to be careful lest we make the passionate watchwords "a passion for souls" and "a passion for Christ" into rival cries. The great passion which the Holy Spirit works in us, whereby He expresses the redemption of our Lord in and through us in practical ways is the passion for Jesus Christ Himself. "You shall be witnesses to Me"—not witnesses only to what Jesus has done or can do, but witnesses who are an infinite satisfaction to His own heart wherever they are placed. The danger in the modern form of Christianity is its departure more and more from the great central figure of the Lord Jesus Christ.

Christian experience does not mean we have thought through the way God works in human lives by His grace, or that we are able to state theologically that God gives the Holy Spirit to those who ask Him—that may be Christian thinking, but it is not Christian experience. Christian experience is living through all this by the marvelous power of the Holy Spirit.

The Holy Spirit working in me does not produce wonderful experiences that make people say, "What a wonderful life that man lives"; the Holy Spirit working in me makes me a passionate, devoted, absorbed lover of the Lord Jesus Christ.

"Passion" is a wonderful word, it is all that we mean by passive suffering and magnificent patience, and spiritually, all that is meant by human passion is lifted to the white, intense, welding heat of enthusiasm for Jesus Christ. God grant that we may be possessed by the Holy Spirit in such fullness that we may be witnesses unto Jesus Christ.

John 7:39; 14:16; 16:24; 20:22, all these references to the Holy Spirit are anticipatory. The Holy Spirit's influence and power were at work before Pentecost, though He was not here. It is not the baptism of the Holy Spirit that changes men, but the power of the ascended Christ coming into men's lives by the Holy Spirit that changes men. The baptism of the Holy Spirit is evidence of the ascended Christ. The Holy Spirit works along the line of the redemption of our Lord, and along that line only. The mighty power of the Holy Spirit brings back to God the experiences of saved men and women, and ultimately if one may put it so, will bring back to God the experiences of a totally redeemed world, a new heaven and a new earth.

"When He has come . . . . He will glorify Me." May God bring straight home to us that no human heart can love the Lord Jesus in the degree that He demands, as in Luke 14:26. There stands the claim of Jesus, tremendously strong; our love for Him must be overwhelmingly more passionate than every devoted earthly relationship. How is it to be done? There is only one lover of the Lord Jesus and that is the Holy Spirit; when we receive the Holy Spirit He turns us into passionate lovers of Jesus Christ. Then out of our lives will flow those rivers of living water that heal and bless, and we spend and suffer and endure in patience all because of one and one only. It is not the passion for men that saves men; the passion for men breaks human hearts. The passion for Christ inwrought by the Holy Spirit is deeper down than the deepest agony the world, the flesh, and the devil can produce. It goes straight down to where our Lord went, and the Holy Spirit works out, not in thinking, but in living, this passion for Jesus Christ in any setting of life any human being indwelt by the Holy Spirit can get into, until Jesus can see of the travail of His soul and be satisfied.

God does not ask us to believe that men can be saved; we cannot pull men out of hell by believing that we can pull them out. When we see a man in hell, every attitude of our souls and minds are paralyzed; we cannot believe he can be saved. God does not ask us to believe that he can be saved; He asks us whether we will believe that Jesus believes He can save him. The facts of life are awful, men's minds are crushed by the terrible facts of evil all around. When the Holy Spirit indwells us, He does not obliterate those facts, but slowly through all the features of crime and evil and wrong, there emerges the one great wonderful figure, the Lord Jesus Christ, and the men possessed by the Holy Spirit, and having the redemption of Christ inwrought in them, say, "Lord, You know," and the saving work goes on.

Galatians 2:20 is not a theological statement, it is a statement of Christian experience wrought by the Holy Spirit. "I am Christ's and He is mine." It is the language of real passion, and it is not too strong an expression for stating the wonderful experience of oneness with Jesus Christ. Paul is so absorbed with Jesus that he does not think of himself apart from this marvelous identification with Jesus Christ. It is closer than a union, it is a oneness illustrated by the vine and the branches. "I am the Vine," not the root, but the vine, "you are the branches." The oneness is as close as that. "One even as We are one."

Paul had one volcanic moment in his life when all his stubbornness was destroyed by the dynamite of the Holy

Spirit. Some folk go through tremendous smashings and break-ings, but there is no need for them to go that way. The great crashings and upsets and disappointments come because of stubbornness. Our great need is to ask for and receive the Holy Spirit in simple faith in the marvelous atonement of Jesus Christ, and He will turn us into passionate lovers of the Lord. It is this passion for Christ worked out in us that makes us witnesses to Jesus wherever we are, men and women in whom He delights, upon whom He can look down with approval; men and women whom He can put in the shadow or the sun; men and women whom He can put upon their beds or on their feet; men and women whom He can send anywhere He chooses. God grant that our watchword may be a "passion for Christ," and that the Holy Spirit may work out in us the experience of Christ being all, so that He may do exactly what He likes with us.

PARTAKERS OF HIS SUFFERINGS

"But rejoice to the extent that you partake of Christ's sufferings" (1 Pet. 4:13).

If we are going to be used by God, He will take us through a multitude of experiences that are not meant for us at all, but meant to make us useful in His hands. There are things we go through which are unexplainable on any other line, and the nearer we get to God the more inexplicable the way seems. It is only on looking back and by getting an explanation from God's Word that we understand His dealings with us. It is part of Christian culture to know what God is after. Jesus Christ suffered "according to the will of God"; He did not suffer in the way we suffer as individuals. In the person of Jesus Christ we have the universal presentation of the whole of the human race.

The Sufferings of the Long Trail of Faith

"But you are those who have continued with Me in My trials" (Luke 22:28).

Jesus Christ looked upon His life as one of temptation; and He goes through the same kind of temptation in us as He went through in the days of His flesh. The essence of Christianity is that we give the Son of God a chance to live and move and have His being in us, and the meaning of all spiritual growth is that He has an increasing opportunity to manifest Himself in our mortal flesh. The temptations of Jesus are not those of a man as man, but the temptations of God as man. "Therefore, in all things He had to be made like His brethren" (Heb. 2:17). Jesus Christ's temptations and ours move in different spheres until we become His brethren by being born from above. "For both He who sanctifies and those who are being sanctified are all of one, for which reason he is not ashamed to call them brethren" (Heb. 2:11). By regeneration the Son of God is formed in me and He has the same setting in my life as He had when on earth. The honor of Jesus Christ is at stake in my bodily life; am I remaining loyal to Him in the temptations which beset His life in me?

Temptation is a shortcut to what is good, not to what is bad. Satan came to our Lord as an angel of light, and all his temptations center around this point—"You are the Son of God, then do God's work in Your own way; put men's needs first, feed them, heal their sicknesses, and they will crown You king." Our Lord would not become king on that line; He deliberately rejected the suggested shortcut, and chose the long trail, evading none of the suffering involved (cf. John 6:15).

"He answered and said, 'It is written, Man shall not live by bread alone, but by every word that proceeds from the mouth of God.'" It is a long time before we are able to listen to every word of God; we listen to one word "bread" when we are hungry, but there is more than that. The fanatic hears only the word of God that comes through the Bible. The word of God comes through the history of the world, through the Christian church, and through nature. We have to learn to live by every word of God, and it takes time. If we try to listen to all the words of God at once, we become surfeited.

The Sorrows of the Long Fear of Hope

"What, could you not watch with Me one hour?" (Matt. 26:40).

Am I watching with Jesus in my life? Am I looking for what He is looking for, or looking for satisfaction for myself? Very few of us watch with Jesus, we have only the idea of His watching with us. He is inscrutable to us because He repre-sents a standard of things that only one or two of us enter into. We are easily roused over things that hurt us; we are scan-dalized at immorality because it upsets us. There is something infinitely more vital than the horror roused by social crimes, and that is the horror of God's Son at sin. In the Garden of Gethsemane the veil is drawn aside, and it reveals the suffering that realizes the horror of sin. Are we more horror-struck by the pride of the human heart against God than we are by the miseries and crimes of human life? That is the test.

"If You are the Son of God throw Yourself down." In effect, "You will win the kingship of men if You do something supernatural, use signs and wonders, bewitch men, and the world will be at Your feet." Jesus said, "It is written again, 'You shall not tempt the LORD your God.'" Are we going to tempt Him again? "If God would only do the magical thing!" We have no right to call on God to do supernatural wonders. The temptation of the church is to go into "show business." When God is working the miracle of His grace in us it is always manifested in a chastened life, utterly restrained. Have I spurned the "long trail" and taken the "shortcut" of self-realization? "Why should I not satisfy myself now? Why should I not do this or that? Why should I not devote myself to the cause I see?" I have no right to identify myself with a cause unless it represents that for which Jesus Christ died. If I allow Jesus Christ to realize Himself in me, I shall not find that I am delivered from temptation, but that I am loosened into it, introduced into what God calls temptation. Am I prepared for God to stamp my personal ambitions right out, prepared for Him to destroy by transfiguration my individual determinations, and bring me into fellowship with the sufferings of His Son? God's purpose is not seen on the surface; it looks as if He is permitting the breaking up of things; but Jesus Christ's hope is that the human race will be as He is Himself, perfectly at one with God. "When the Son of Man comes, will He really find faith on the earth?"

The Strain of the Last Terror of Love

"Who is My mother?" (Matt. 12:46–50).

"Behold your mother!" (John 19:25–27).

The greatest benefits God has conferred on human life—fatherhood, motherhood, childhood, home—become the greatest curse if Jesus Christ is not the head. A home that does not acknowledge Jesus Christ as the head will become exclusive on the line of its own affinities; related to Jesus Christ, the home becomes a center for all the benedictions of motherhood and sonhood to be expressed to everyone, "an open house for the universe." By His death and resurrection our Lord has the right to give eternal life to every man; by His ascension He enters heaven and keeps the door open for humanity.

Through the travail of the nations just now the Spirit of God is working out His own purpose; no nation is exclusively God's. When the Holy Spirit enters a man, instantly he feels called to be a missionary; he has had introduced into him the very nature of God which is focused in John 3:16 "God so loved the world . . . ." The Holy Spirit sheds abroad in our hearts the love of God, a love which breaks all confines of body, soul, and spirit. The Holy Spirit severs human connections and makes connections which are universal—a complete union of men and women all over the world in a bond in which there is no snare. God's call is for *the world*; the question of location is a matter of the engineering of God's providence.

Some things work suddenly and are seen; others, such as the life in a seed, work slowly and silently. There are some points of view which we do not see but they see us; that is, they take us into themselves; and some points of God's truth are like that. You say, "I don't understand this" because you are part of it. We do not take God into our consciousness: God takes us into His consciousness, and that means we are taken up into His purpose, not into conscious agreement with His purpose; there is always more than we are conscious of. God's order comes to us in the haphazard. Things look as if they happen by chance, but behind all is the purpose of God, and the New Testament reveals what that purpose is. We are made partakers of Christ's sufferings; then, says Peter, rejoice, because when His glory is revealed you will be glad also with exceeding joy.

There is no snare of pride along any of these lines because there is no aim of our own in them; there is only the aim of God.

THE THEOLOGY OF REST

Mark 4:35–41

"Come to Me . . . and I will give you rest," that is, build you up into a stable life in which there is neither weariness nor cessation from activities. The Bible never glorifies our natural conception of things; it does not use the words "rest" and "joy" and "peace" as we use them, and our common-sense interpretation of words must be keyed up to the way God uses them, otherwise we lose the "humor" of God.

The incident recorded in Mark 4:35–41 is not an incident in the life of a man, but in the life of God as man. This man asleep in the boat is God incarnate. Jesus had said to the disciples, "Let us cross over to the other side," but when the storm arose, instead of relying upon Him, they failed Him. The actual circumstances were so crushing that their common sense was up in alarm, their panic carried them off their feet, and in terror they awoke Him. When we are in fear, we can do nothing less than pray to God, but our Lord has the right to expect of those who name His Name and have His nature in them an understanding confidence in Him. Instead of that, when we are at our wits' end we go back to the elementary prayers of those who do not know Him, and prove that we have not the slightest atom of confidence in Him and in His government of the world: He is asleep—the tiller is not in His hand, and we sit down in nervous dread. God expects His children to be so confident in Him that in a crisis they are the ones upon whom He can rely. A great point is reached spiritually when we stop worrying God over personal matters or over any matter. God expects of us the one thing that glorifies Him—and that is to remain absolutely confident in Him, remembering what He has said beforehand, and sure that His purposes will be fulfilled.

Always beware of the thing that shuts you up but does not convince you—common sense will do that. What is common sense worth in such a crisis as is symbolized here? It simply disturbs God. In this incident our Lord answered the disciples' cry, but He rebuked them for their lack of faith, "Why are you so fearful? How is it that you have no faith?" What a pang must have shot through their hearts—"Missed it again!" And what a pang will come through our hearts when we realize we have done the same thing, when we might have produced downright joy in the heart of Jesus by remaining absolutely confident in Him, no matter what was ahead. The joy that a believer can give to God is the purest pleasure God ever allows a saint, and it is very humiliating to realize how little joy we do give Him. We put our trust in God up to a certain point, then we say, "Now I must do my best." There are times when there is no human best to be done, when the divine best must be left to work, and God expects those of us who know Him to be confident in His ability and power. We have to learn what these fishermen learned, that the carpenter of Nazareth knew better than they did how to manage the boat. Is Jesus Christ a carpenter, or is He God to me? If He is only man, why let Him take the tiller of the boat? Why pray to Him? But if He be God, then be heroic enough to go to the breaking point and not break in your confidence in Him.

If we have faith at all it must be faith in Almighty God; when He has said a thing, He will perform it; we have to remain steadfastly obedient to Him. Are we learning to be silent before God, or are we worrying Him with needless prayers? In this terrific crisis of war many of us have lost our wits, we see only breakers ahead, with nothing for us to do but watch the whole thing go to ruin; and yet He said, "Let us cross over to the other side." Just as a general looks for the man who keeps his head in the fight, so the Lord looks for the man who will keep his faith in Him. "When the Son of Man comes, will He really find faith on the earth?" (Luke 18:8). There is no more glorious opportunity than the day in which we live for proving in personal life and in every way that we are confident in God.

The stars do their work without fuss; God does His work without fuss, and saints do their work without fuss. The people who are always desperately active are a nuisance; it is through the saints who are one with Him that God is doing things all the time. The broken and the jaded and the twisted are being ministered to by God through the saints who are not overcome by their own panic, who because of their oneness with Him are absolutely at rest, consequently He can work through them. A sanctified saint remains perfectly confident in God, because sanctification is not something the Lord gives me, sanctification is *Himself in me*. There is only one holiness, the holiness of God, and only one sanctification, the sanctification that has its origin in Jesus Christ. "But of Him you are in Christ Jesus, who became for us . . . sanctification" (1 Cor. 1:30). A sanctified saint is at leisure from himself and his own affairs, confident that God is bringing all things out well.

Spiritual realities can always be counterfeited. "Rest in the LORD" can be turned into pious "rust" in sentiment. What is all our talk about sanctification going to amount to? It should amount to that rest in God which means a oneness with Him such as Jesus had—not only blameless in God's sight, but a deep joy to Him. God grant we may be.

THE ALTAR OF FELLOWSHIP

"For we do not want you to be ignorant, brethren, of our trouble which came to us in Asia . . ." (2 Cor. 1:8).

Human fellowship can go to great lengths, but not all the way. Fellowship with God can go all lengths. The apostle Paul literally fulfilled what we mean by this phrase, the altar of fellowship; he offered himself liberally and freely to God, and then offered himself at the hands of God, freely and fully, for the service of God among men, whether or not men understood him. "And I will very gladly spend and be spent for your souls; though the more abundantly I love you, the less I am loved" (2 Cor. 12:15). Do we know anything about this altar of fellowship whereby we offer back to God the best He has given us, and then let Him reoffer it as broken bread and poured-out wine to His other children?

Disasters of Fellowship

". . . so that we despaired even of life." (2 Cor. 1:8).

There are disasters to be faced by the one who is in real fellowship with the Lord Jesus Christ. God has never promised to keep us immune from trouble; He says, "I will be with him in trouble," which is a very different thing. Paul was "an apostle of Jesus Christ by the will of God," and it is this fact

that accounts for the crushing criticism and the spiteful treat-
ment to which he was subjected by those who could not discern on what authority he based his apostleship. Paul was a
Pharisee of the Pharisees, he stood in the fore rank of learning
until Jesus appeared to him, staggered him, blinded him, extin-
guished all his personal aims, and sent him out to be an apostle
to the Gentiles—"I have chosen him." That was the ground
Paul stood on, and that only—he was an apostle *by the will of
God*" (see Gal. 1:15–16).

If you are experiencing the disasters of fellowship, don't
get into despair, remain unswervingly and unhesitatingly faithful to the Lord Jesus Christ and refuse to compromise for one
second. Don't say "it can't be done" because you see a thing is
going to crush your physical life. Calculate on the disaster of
fellowship, because through it God is going to bring you into
fellowship with His Son. This is also true of work for God—
"except a grain of wheat falls into the ground and dies . . . ."

Discipline of Fellowship

"Yes, we had the sentence of death in ourselves." (2 Cor.
1:9).

If I am in fellowship with Jesus Christ and am indwelt by
Him, I have the answer of death in myself, and nothing the
world, the flesh, or the devil can do can touch me. This divine
light came to Paul out of his desperate experience in Ephesus;
he realized then that nothing could any more frighten him. The
discipline of fellowship brought about in Paul's experience the
assimilation of what he believed. We say many things which
we believe, but they have never been tested. Discipline has to
come through all the things we believe in order to turn them
into real spiritual possessions. It is the trial of our faith that is
precious. "Hang in" to Jesus Christ against all odds until He

turns your spiritual beliefs into real possessions. It is heroism to believe in God.

Devotion of Fellowship

". . . that we should not trust in ourselves" (2 Cor. 1:9).

Whenever we begin to note where we are successful for God, we do trust in ourselves. In Luke 10:20 our Lord says, in effect, "Don't rejoice in successful service, but rejoice that you are rightly related to Me." The Lord Jesus Christ is the beginning, the middle, and the end. Many are willing to accept sanctification, but they do not want the one who is sanctification. "I am looking to see whether I am a blessing." Suppose Paul had looked to see the result of his work among the Corinthians! It seemed disaster all along the line. The devotion of fellowship means we are persuaded, like Paul, that "neither death nor life . . . nor any other created thing, shall be able to separate us from the love of God which is in Christ Jesus our Lord." God has become to us the one vital reality.

The Declaration of Fellowship

". . . but in God who raises the dead" (2 Cor. 1:9).

"According to my earnest expectation and hope, . . . Christ will be magnified in my body" (Phil. 1:20). Paul argues—"whether by life or by death," no matter! He trusts in God, and knows He will do all He intends to do through him, and that nothing and no one can thwart His purpose.

Do I know anything about the altar of fellowship? Am I related to things, whether they be disastrous or delightful, from the standpoint of my oneness with the Lord Jesus Christ? The one dominating enthusiasm of the apostle Paul's life was his personal, passionate devotion to Jesus Christ. "In all these things we are more than conquerors through Him who loved us."

THE EVENING TEST OF LOYALTY

"For Joab had defected to Adonijah, though he had not defected to Absalom" (1 Kings 2:28).

Is there an equivalent to this in your life? Do you find you are turning away from loyalty to Jesus for some insignificant thing? There was a time when you stood magnificently for God, days when heart and brain and body were ablaze in absolute devotion to Jesus Christ, you would have gone anywhere for Him. The prince of this world came and found nothing in you in those days; the lusts of the world found you adamant. Has God been lifting the veil and do you find the enthusiasm is gone, the great passionate devotion to Jesus is gone? The prince of this world has begun to find something in you at last, and what a miserably insignificant thing it is that has turned you! The reason you are not so zealous for the glory of God as you used to be, not so keen about the habits of your spiritual life, is because you have imperceptibly begun to surrender morally.

Beware of the Spiritual Undertime

"Stand fast therefore in the liberty by which Christ has made us free, and do not be entangled again with a yoke of bondage" (Gal. 5:1).

Joab stood the big test and was not turned by the fascinations of Absalom, but towards the end of his life he was turned by the craven Adonijah. Always remain alert to the fact that where anyone has gone back is exactly where we all may go back. ("Therefore let him who thinks he stands take heed lest he fall.") You have borne the burden and heat of the day, been through the big test, now beware of the undertime, the afterpart of the day spiritually. We are apt to forget that there is always an afterwards, and that it comes close on the heels of the present. You made a big break with all that Absalom represents, and you are apt to say nothing will have any effect on you now, but it certainly will. You stood the big test with Absalom; don't turn after Adonijah. It is in the aftermath of a great spiritual transaction that the "retired sphere of the leasts" begins to sap. "Now that I have been through the supreme crisis, it is not in the least likely that I shall turn to the things of the world." It is the least likely thing that is the peril. The Bible characters never fell on their weak points but on their strong ones; unguarded strength is double weakness. It is in the afterpart of the day spiritually that we have to be alert. This does not mean that you are to be morbidly introspective, looking forward with dread, but that you keep alert; don't forecast where the temptation will come. One of the best things for your spiritual welfare is to keep recounting the wonders God has done for you, record them in a book; mark the passage in your Bible and continually refer to it, keep it fresh in your mind. Thomas Boston used to pray, "O Lord, keep me strong in the sense of Thy call." We do not keep the ideal of our attachment to Jesus constantly enough before us.

Be Alert for the Spiritual Undertow

"You ran well. Who hindered you . . . ?" (Gal. 5:7).

An undertow is an undercurrent flowing in a different

direction from the water at the surface. It is the undercurrent that drowns; a swimmer will never plunge into an undercurrent, a fool will. The spiritual undertow that switched away the Galatians was Judaism, formalism. It was not dominant, but hidden; it ran in exactly the opposite direction to the current of liberty into which they were being brought by Christ. Instead of going out to sea, out into the glorious liberty of the children of God, they were being switched away. "You ran well . . . ." They had been heading straight for the ocean, but the undercurrent of ritualism bewitched them, hindered them from obeying the truth. After a big transaction with God the current of your life heads you straight out to sea, right over the harbor bar, every sail set; now be alert for the spiritual undertow that would suck you back. The undercurrent is always most dangerous just where the river merges with the sea. The undercurrent is of the same nature as the river and will take you back into its swirling current; not out into the main stream, but back to the shipwrecks on the bank. The most pitiable of all wrecks are those inside the harbor.

Now that you have been swept out into the realization of God's purpose, be alert over the things which used to be strong in the upper reaches of your life. The surface current, the current in which God has set your life, is the most powerful; but be alert for the spiritual undertow, the current that sets in another direction. It is after the floodtide of a spiritual transaction that the undertow begins to tell, and to tell terribly. The undercurrent for each one of us is different. It is only felt at certain stages of the tide; when the tide is full there is no undercurrent.

Be Careful of the Spiritual Undertone

"For Demas has forsaken me, having loved this present world . . ." (2 Tim. 4:10).

In music an undertone is a tone not quite in tune. When waves occur in a chord it is because the organ or piano is a half semi-tone out of tune. The Vox Humana stop, which gives the effect of the human voice, is tuned a half semi-tone flat to the rest of the notes, which accounts for the peculiar wave, almost a discord. It is the same spiritually. As you listen carefully to the music God is producing in your life, is there an undertone, something not in full harmony, a least thing, that you will not detect unless you are spiritually expert? The undertone was represented in Demas by his love of the world. Earlier Paul had referred to him with joy as "my fellow laborer" (Philem. 24), but now the undertone of worldliness has begun to tell and is switching him off. The undertone in music is the fascinating thing that lends bewitchment; and spiritually it is the under- tone that puts the tiniest tang of danger into the life. Be careful of it. The least likely thing is that we should turn away from God, but it is the least likely thing that will trip us up if we are not warned.

You have been having big transactions with God and are being taken right out into the purpose of God, now beware of the undertime, the after-part of the spiritual day. You have remained true to God under great tests, now be alert over the least things. "Mighty events turn on a straw" (Carlyle). To be forewarned is to be forearmed. The way to keep alert is to keep your memory bright before God; ask Him never to allow you to forget what you have been in relation to Him. Is God saying to you, "You are not in love with Me now, but I remember the time when you were; I remember the love of your betrothal?" If you find as you recall what God remembers about you, that He is not what He used to be to you, let it produce shame and humiliation, because that shame will bring the godly sorrow that works repentance. Don't merely accept the rebuke— receive it, and alter your conduct at once. Our only safety is to abide in Him. "Kept by the power of God."

THE DISCIPLINE OF DISILLUSIONMENT

Isaiah 38:15–20

To be disillusioned means that for us there are no more false appearances in life. A disillusioned person, although all he says may be correct, is often cynical and unkindly severe about other people. The disillusionment which comes from God is just as accurate and clear and understanding, but there is no cynicism in it. "But Jesus did not commit Himself to them . . . for He knew what was in man" (John 2:24–25).

The discipline of disillusionment brings us to the place where we see men and women as they are, and yet there is no cynicism, we have no stinging, bitter things to say. Many of the cruel things in life spring from the fact that we will suffer from illusions, we are not true to one another as facts, we are only true to our ideas of one another. Everything is either delightful and fine, or else mean and dastardly, according to our own ideas. Jesus Christ is the master of the human soul, He knows what is in the human heart (see Mark 7:21–22), and He has no illusions about any man.

Few of us believe what Jesus Christ says, we prefer to trust our illusion of innocence. When we trust our own innocence, we enthrone our illusion and discard Jesus Christ, and it is likely that something will happen to awaken us to the fact that what Jesus Christ says is true. If we give our hearts to Him to be kept, we need never know this experientially. A certain type of innocence is culpable. Innocence is the characteristic of a child, but innocence in a man or woman is culpable and wrong. It means that their own whiteness is so guarded that they are unfit for life. Men and women must be pure and virtuous, and virtue is always the outcome of conflict.

Most of the suffering in human life comes because we refuse to be disillusioned. For instance, if I love a human being, and do not love God, I demand of that man or woman an infinite satisfaction which they cannot give. I demand of them every perfection and every rectitude, and when I do not get it, I become cruel and vindictive and jealous. Think of the average married life after, say, five or ten years; too often it sinks down into the most commonplace drudgery. The reason is that the husband and wife have not known God rightly, they have not gone through the transfiguration of love, nor entered through the discipline of disillusionment into satisfaction in God, and consequently they have begun to endure one another instead of having one another for enjoyment in God. The human heart must have satisfaction, but there is only one being who can satisfy the last aching abyss of the human heart, and that is our Lord Jesus Christ. That is why He is apparently so severe in regard to every human relationship. He says if we are going to be His disciples, occasion may arise when we must hate both father and mother, and every closest tie there is. Our Lord has no illusions about men, and He knows that every relationship in life that is not based on loyalty to Him will end in disaster.

In Rectitude Through Suffering

"I shall walk carefully [so in solemn procession—R.V. marg.] all my years" (v. 15).

A peculiar nobility, a stately element, comes into the life that has had to face death; that man sees things in their real perspective. It is through suffering that we are disillusioned, but selfish suffering does not disillusionize. A man may be perfected through suffering or be made worse through suffering, it depends on his disposition. Am I in the place of disillusionment, or have I refused to be disillusioned when God has tried to talk to me through difficulties and in sufferings? If I have, it is a sign that I am still suffering from illusions; I am still culpably innocent. God is not to blame; I am to blame.

The moral caliber of a man shows itself in the way he conducts himself in the shallow things of life. Our lives are divided into two domains, the shallow and the profound. Jesus Christ was considered to be so shallow by the religious people of His day that they said He was a gluttonous man and a wine-bibber. His was such a full-orbed natural life that no attention was paid to Him, He was easily ignored and made of no account. Men were blind to the real profundity of His life. Our profound, solitary life is with God alone, and we have no business to obtrude it before others, unless God is bringing them there too. The shallow means the actual surface life we all live with one another. Am I prepared to let God dominate both the shallow and the profound?

The test of our spiritual life is how we behave when we ought to be shallow for God. It is easy to behave at a prayer meeting; it takes all the grace of God to behave at a marriage feast. We must not obtrude the prayer meeting conduct into the shallow things. We have to carry out our relationship with God in the shallow things, without any illusions.

No one ever became spiritual without being fanatical for a season. The shallow intercourse of our lives falls away and people object to us, because, if we are right, they are wrong. It is the swing of the pendulum to the opposite extreme of what the life used to be. My "right hand" is the thing that makes me delightful to other people, yet Jesus Christ says, "If your right hand causes you to sin, cut it off." The maimed stage is only for a season; the example for a Christian is not a maimed life, but the life of the Lord Jesus Christ (see Matt. 5:29–30, 48).

In Realization Through Salvation

"You have lovingly delivered my soul from the pit" (v. 17).

This is the greatest revelation that ever struck the human life, namely, that God loves the sinner. God so loved the world when it was sinful that He sent His Son to die for it. Our Lord has no illusions about any of us. He sees every man and woman as the descendants of Adam who sinned, and with capacities in our hearts of which we have no idea. Natural ability has nothing to do with fitness for God's salvation, it may have to do with fitness for Christian work, that is a matter of civilization.

Hezekiah begins to see himself exactly as he is in God's sight. When once a man has been "undressed" by the Holy Spirit, he will never be able to despair of anyone else. External sins are to a large extent the accident of upbringing, but when the Spirit of God comes in and probes to the depths and reveals the disposition of sin, we begin to understand what salvation is. God cannot take anything from the sinner but his solid sin, otherwise salvation would have no meaning for him (see 2 Cor. 5:21).

Have I realized disillusionment through salvation? Think of the worst man or woman you know; do you believe that that one can be presented perfect in Jesus Christ? If you do not, it is because you are still under an illusion about yourself, you still have a notion that there is something in your virtues that will save you. There are men and women, such as the rich young ruler and Mary of Bethany, who are utterly unsullied until they receive the Spirit of God, and then a remarkable thing happens—the corruption to themselves of their natural virtues. It is a difficult thing to state because so few try to state it. When someone who is possessed of patience naturally is born again, he becomes impatient; or if someone has been pure and upright and worthy naturally, he may begin to have thoughts of evil such as he never dreamed of before. Our natural virtues break down because they are not promises of what we are going to be, but remnants of what we once were, remnants of the man God made and sin ruined. Jesus Christ does not patch up our natural virtues. He creates a new man, "Therefore, if anyone is in Christ, he is a new creation; old things have passed away; behold, all things have become new" (2 Cor. 5:17), and we find that every virtue we possess, is His alone.

Jesus Christ cannot be spoken of in terms of the natural virtues, as a patient man, or a pure, noble man. He is the "man from heaven," the full-orbed man, and the New Testament says we have to live as He lived. Our old way of reasoning and looking at things must go, and all things must become new. The way we act when we come up against things proves whether we have been disillusioned or not; do we trust in our wits or do we worship God? If we trust in our wits, God will have to repeat the same lesson until we learn it. Whenever our faith is not in God, and in Him alone, there is still an illusion somewhere.

In Revelation Through Submission

"Those who go down to the pit cannot hope for Your truth" (v. 18).

Submission does not mean that I submit to the power of God because I must. A stoic submits without passion, that is slavery; a saint sees God's will and submits to it with a passionate love, and in his daily life exhibits his love to God to whom he has submitted. The real meaning of submission is seen in the Sermon on the Mount. Jesus says that if you are rightly related to God, you should show that relationship to men; submit enough to live it out in your daily life. It will mean that you do not take the law into your own hands, you do not refuse to be hit. You never need be hit or hurt, but every time you refuse to be, your Lord takes the blow. Think of the honor our Lord confers on us; we have the power to prevent Him being stabbed by taking the stab ourselves. "I now rejoice in my sufferings for you, and fill up in my flesh what is lacking in the afflictions of Christ, for the sake of His body, which is the church" (Col. 1:24). When someone over-reaches us, every logical power in us says, resent it. Morally speaking we should, but Jesus Christ says that if we are His disciples, we will go the second mile; as soon as we do, men will cast out our names as evil, as He said they would.

Until we are rightly related to God, we deify courage and heroism. We will do anything that is heroic, anything that puts the inspiration of strain on us; but when it comes to submitting to being a weak thing for God, it takes Almighty God to do it. "We are weak in Him." Some of us have still to go through disillusionment on this line, we have not learned to submit, we prefer to stand on our rights. "Take My yoke upon you and learn from Me," says Jesus. Am I loyal to Him, or am I clinging to my own rights? Is my tongue God's, or is there the poison of asps under it?

In Rejoicing Through Sacrifice

"Therefore we will sing my songs with stringed instruments all the days of our life, in the house of the LORD" (v. 20).

Hezekiah is not lying in a stately armchair with a sentimental atmosphere around him, he is still sick with a boil, but he says, "I will offer to You the sacrifice of thanksgiving." Praising costs. If you are in the dumps, sing! Sacrifice means giving up something that we mind giving up. We talk of giving up our possessions; none of them are ours to give up. "One's life does not consist in the abundance of the things he possesses." Our Lord tells us to give up the one thing that is going to hurt badly, that is, our right to ourselves.

Jesus Christ taught a kind of "hypocrisy" to His disciples! "But you, when you fast, anoint your head and wash your face, so that you do not appear to men to be fasting." Don't say you are fasting, or that you spent the night in prayer, wash your face; and never let your dearest friend know what you put yourself through. Natural stoicism was created by God, and when it is transfigured by the indwelling Holy Spirit, people will never think of you. "He must increase, but I must decrease." John is not saying that with a quivering mouth, or out of modesty; he is expressing the spiritual delight of his life. I am to decrease because He has come! He says it with a manly thrill. Is Jesus Christ increasing in my life, or am I taking everything for myself? When I get disillusioned I see Him and Him alone, there are no illusions left. It is a matter of indifference how I am hurt, the one thing I am concerned about is that every man may be presented "perfect in Christ Jesus."

DID JESUS CHRIST COME FOR PEACE?

"His name will be called . . . Prince of Peace" (Isa. 9:6).

The Christmas Message

"Glory to God in the highest, and on earth peace, good will toward men!" (Luke 2:14).

Not a prophecy but a proclamation.

The average views of Christianity seem to be right until they are made explicit. For instance, the average view that Christianity stands for peace, for the brotherhood of men, for the peace and prosperity of nations is true generally speaking; but if you look at it narrowly you will find there is a great deal that does not fit into that view, and the critic (not necessarily a clever critic, but a man with an open mind, facing things as they are today) asks, "What does it all amount to? Twenty centuries have passed since Jesus, the Prince of Peace, came and the angels prophesied peace on earth, but where is peace?" The New Testament does not say that the angels prophesied peace: they proclaimed peace—"on earth peace among men in whom He is well pleased,"(KJV) that is, peace to men of goodwill towards God. Jesus Christ came to manifest that God was with man, "and they shall call His name Immanuel, which is translated, 'God with us.' " Jesus Christ is a unique being—God-man, and by Him any man can be made a son of God according to the pattern of Jesus Christ. This is the Christian revelation. Jesus says, "Come to Me," and when a man does come to Jesus he is born into another domain and his whole outlook is altered. Deliverance from sin is only part of the meaning of being born from above, the reason it is so important to us is because we are sinners; but the meaning of new birth from God's side is that a man is brought into the viewpoint of His Son. The Christmas message crystallizes the whole thing: "that holy One who is to be born will be called the Son of God." God manifest in the flesh is what has become profoundly possible for any man on the basis of redemption.

The Christ Menace

"Do not think that I came to bring peace on earth. I did not come to bring peace but a sword" (Matt. 10:34).

Not a propaganda but a personal power.

Is that the average view of what Jesus Christ came to do? The average view is that He came as a meek and mild and gently dispositioned person to spread peace and love all around and to make life infinitely more beautiful. But Jesus says here that we are not to allow ourselves to think that that is what He came to do; He did not come to fling peace abroad indiscriminately. He came to send a sword. We build our ideas on what we are taught about Jesus Christ, not on what the New Testament says. We are taught that Jesus Christ was meek and loving, and He was; but we forget the times when He was ablaze with zeal for His Father's honor. In the temple instead of seeing a "meek and mild and gentle Jesus," we see a terrible being with a whip of small cords in His hand, driving out the moneychangers. "I am gentle and lowly in heart," says Jesus, but His meekness was towards God, not towards men. God the Father could do what He liked with His Son, and the Son received with absolute meekness the dispensations of the Father.

"I did not come to bring peace but a sword." As soon as the Holy Spirit brings you face to face with a presentation of truth which you never saw before, your peace is gone, and instead there is the sword of conviction. The coming of Jesus Christ is not a peaceful thing, it is a disturbing thing, because it means the destruction of every peace that is not based on a personal relationship to Himself. If once the moral equilibrium has been upset by conviction of sin, holiness is the only result or no peace for ever. "I was alive once without the law," says Paul. When a man comes to see what Jesus Christ demands, his peace of mind is upset. "If I had not come and spoken to them, they would have no sin." Then why did He come? People say "The Sermon on the Mount is good enough for me" (I should think it was!), "but I do not see the need for preaching the atonement and the cross of Christ." But where are you going to begin to be what the Sermon on the Mount says you must be? Jesus Christ's demand is that we be as holy as He is Himself, that we reach the "whiter than snow-shine" in our conduct, that we are unfathomably pure in heart. Are you so pure in heart that you never lust, never have a thought in the background of your mind that God could censure? If all Jesus Christ came to do was to put before us an ideal we cannot attain, we are happier without knowing it. But Jesus Christ did not come primarily to teach: He came to put within us His own disposition, that is, the Holy Spirit, whereby we can live a totally new life. By conviction of sin a man is probed wide awake and made to realize that he needs to be regenerated; when he gets there, Jesus says, "Blessed are you." The one essential thing which makes a man a Christian is not what he believes in his head but what he is in disposition. Jesus Christ comes to the central part of a man's life, and the bedrock of Christianity is that Jesus Christ has done something for me I could not do for myself. Christianity is not merely adherence to a set of principles or to a plan of salvation, but a personal relationship to Jesus Christ; consequently the spontaneous working of the Holy Spirit in a man may make him appear inconsistent. A Christian is not consistent to hard and fast creeds, he is consistent only to the life of the Son of God in him.

The Christian Meaning

"Therefore, if anyone is in Christ, he is a new creation" (2 Cor. 5:17).

Not a preaching but a purity.

If we are saved by the grace of God it means not only that we are delivered from destruction, but that we are a new creation. The condemnation is to know a thing and not work it out. We know we have experienced the grace of God, but are we living the life of regeneration in our actual experience? We take the Christian view up to a certain point and exploit it according to our belief. The average Christian says, "Oh, yes, I am saved." Well, produce your goods! Where are the characteristics in you that Jesus Christ taught us to expect in a Christian? In what way are you different from other men? Are you just as hard in driving a bargain as they are? If Christianity does not affect my money and my marriage relationships, it is not worth anything. Today men are asking not so much if Christianity is true, but if it is real? Does it amount to anything in actual life? If I have a personal relationship to Jesus on the basis of His redemption, it will show in the way I live, in the way I act towards men; "old things have passed away; behold, all things have become new."

Did Jesus Christ come for peace? He did; but it is a peace that is characteristic of Himself, not peace at any price. "My peace I give to you." The peace that Jesus gives is never engineered by circumstances on the outside; it is a peace based on a personal relationship that holds all through. "In the world you will have tribulation, in Me, peace."

Oh, the peace my Savior gives,
Peace I never knew before,

is a biblical thought. That peace is the deepest thing a human personality can experience, it is almighty, a peace that passes all understanding.

SPIRITUAL EDUCATION

"In your patience possess your souls" (Luke 21:19).

Education is a bringing out of what is there and giving it the power of expression, not packing in what does not belong; and spiritual education means learning how to give expression to the divine life that is in us when we are born from above.

"In your patience possess your souls," said Jesus to His disciples. Soul is the expression of my personal spirit in my body, the way I reason and think and act, and Jesus taught that a man must lose his soul in order to gain it; he must lose absolutely his own way of reasoning and looking at things, and begin to estimate from an entirely different standpoint. We have the Spirit of Jesus gifted to us, but we have to form the mind which was also in Christ Jesus. No man has the mind of Christ unless he has acquired it.

Dimensions of Divine Love

"For God so loved the world that He gave His only begotten Son . . ." (John 3:16).

". . . the width and length and depth and height—to know the love of Christ which passes knowledge . . ." (Eph. 3:18–19).

The first thing we need to be educated in spiritually is a

71

knowledge of the dimensions of divine love, its length and depth and width and height. That God is love is a revelation. Unless I am born from above, what is the use of telling me God is love? To me He is not love. Where is the love of God in war? in suffering? in all the inevitable inequalities of life? No one who faces facts as they are could ever prove that God is love unless he accepts the revelation of His love made by Jesus Christ. John 3:16 does not begin to have any meaning to the natural man who knows nothing whatever of the domain Jesus Christ represents; but let him come up against things and be brought to his wits' end, and then let him read John 3:16. Not until we realize that there is something tragic at the basis of human life shall we recognize the love of God.

In the cross we may see the dimensions of divine love. The cross is not the cross of a man, but the exhibition of the heart of God. At the back of the wall of the world stands God with His arms outstretched, and every man driven there is driven into the arms of God. The cross of Jesus is the supreme evidence of the love of God (Rom. 8:35–39). "Who shall separate us from the love of Christ?" (v. 35).

The cross of Christ reveals that the blazing center of the love of God is the holiness of God, not His kindness and compassion. If the divine love pretends I am all right when I am all wrong, then I have a keener sense of justice than the Almighty. God is a holy God, and the marvel of the redemption is that God the holy One puts into me, the unholy one, a new disposition, the disposition of His Son.

Direction of Divine Living

1 Corinthians 13:4–8

Love is the sovereign preference of my person for another person, and Jesus demands that that other person be Himself;

and the direction of divine living is that I deliberately identify myself with Jesus Christ's interests in other people.

"Love suffers long and is kind; love does not envy; love . . . does not seek its own, is not provoked, thinks no evil; . . . bears all things, believes all things, hopes all things, endures all things. Love never fails." That is Christian living in actual life. If I have the disposition of a fault-finder, I am a most uncomfortable person to live with, but if the love of God has been shed abroad in my heart, I begin to see extraordinary self-sacrifice under the roughest of exteriors. I begin to see nobility where before I only saw meanness, because I see only what I bring with me the power of seeing—a most humiliating thing to realize!

The direction of divine living is that I identify myself with God's interests in other people, and He is interested in some funny people, namely, you and me! We see the humor of our heavenly Father in the way He brings around us the type of people who are to us what we have been to Him; now He will watch how we behave to them. How did Jesus treat us? With infinite patience, with amplitude of forgiveness and generosity. Then He says that we are to treat them in the same way. "But if you do not forgive men their trespasses, neither will your Father forgive your trespasses."

Never try to be right with an abstract enemy, but get right with the enemy you have got. It is easy to talk about loving the heathen; never go off on the abstract. The direction of divine living is that I have to be as kind to others as God has been to me, not the others I have not met, but those I have met. ". . . that ye may be the sons of your Father which is in heaven."

Another direction of divine living is the realizing that a Christian has the right not to insist on his rights; this is only learned by the sharpest and most severe lessons. In the Sermon on the Mount our Lord teaches us not to look for justice, but never to cease to give it. That is not common sense, it is either madness or Christianity. To look for justice is to educate my-self not in the practice of divine living, but in my "divine" right to myself. Beware of looking to see where other people come short. God expects us to be exactly what we know the other person should be; when we realize that, we will stop criticizing and having a measuring rod for other people.

When the love of God is in me I must learn how to let it express itself; I must educate myself in the matter; it takes time. "Acquire your soul with patience," says Jesus. Never give way to this spirit—"Oh, well, I have fallen again, I will stay down now." Have patience with yourself, and remember that this is salvation not for the hereafter, but for here and now.

Discipline of Divine Loyalty

"Do you love me? . . . Feed My sheep" (John 21:15–17).

Is that what we have been doing, feeding Jesus Christ's sheep? Take a rapid survey. Have we been nourishing the lives of people in the understanding of Jesus, or has our aim been to maintain our particular deposit of doctrine? According to Jesus, divine loyalty means that we feed His sheep in the knowledge of Him, not feed them with our doctrine. Peter had boasted earlier of his love for Jesus—"Even if all are made to stumble because of You, I will never be made to stumble." But there is no brag left in him now— "Lord, You know all things; You know that I love You." "Feed My sheep." The discipline of divine loyalty is not that I am true to a doctrine, but so true to Jesus that other people are nourished in the knowledge of Him. Get rid of the idea that you must do good things, and remember what Jesus says, "He who believes in

Me, . . . out of his heart will flow rivers of living water." In the Christian life it is never "Do, do," but "Be, be, and I will do through you." The type of man produced by the Spirit of Jesus is the one who bears a growing family likeness to Jesus.

Am I getting nobler, better, more helpful, more humble, as I get older? Am I exhibiting the life that men take knowledge of as having been with Jesus, or am I getting more self-assertive, more deliberately determined to have my own way? It is a great thing to tell yourself the truth.

There are some of the lines of spiritual education: learning the dimensions of divine love, that the center of that love is holiness; that the direction of divine living is a deliberate surrender of our own point of view in order to learn Jesus Christ's point of view, and seeing that men and women are nourished in the knowledge of Jesus. The only way that can be done is by being loyal to Jesus myself.

THE MAKEUP OF A WORKER

2 Timothy 1:12–17

The Service of Memory

"Then last of all He was seen by me also, as by one born out of due time" (1 Cor. 15:8).

"For you have heard of my former conduct . . . how I persecuted the church of God beyond measure . . ." (Gal. 1:13).

Paul refers to himself as "one born out of due time." Every worker for God has that feeling about himself—"If only I had known this before"; or, "If only I had made better use of my time." There is always the feeling that we have certain drawbacks. These thoughts continually recur on the threshold of the mind of the worker, and they have to be overcome. The only way we can serve God is by having "no confidence in the flesh."

When Paul says "forgetting those things which are behind," he is not referring to his past life; Paul never forgot that he had been "a blasphemer, a persecutor, and an insolent man;" but he determinedly forgot all he had attained to in the Christian life, because he was always pressing on to "those things which are ahead." The gospel of the grace of God takes the stain of memory from a worker, not by making him ignore the past, but by enabling him to see that God can make it of service in his work for God. A worker should never tell people to forget the past; preachers of the "gospel of temperament" do that. If we forget the past we will be hard and obtuse. If we are hard, we are of no use to God; and unless we know the cross of Christ as the power which takes the stinging stain out of memory and transforms it, we are of no use to others. Unless a worker has had the experience of the grace of God transform-ing the stain of memory into a personal experience of salvation, there will be a weak-kneed-ness and a feeble-handed-ness about him that will hinder God's message. If there is no sense of sin, no stain in memory to be transformed, the trend of the teaching is apt to be the line of higher education and culture and rarely the great line Paul was always on. The gospel can never be preached by sinless lips, but only by the lips of those who have been saved from sin by the atonement. Angels can-not preach the gospel, only beings such as Paul and you and I can preach the gospel. We say that Jesus preached the gospel, but He did more: He came that there might be a gospel to preach.

The first element in the makeup of a worker is that he knows the service of memory, not a memory of things that he can excuse, but a memory out of which God has taken the sting, so that he is in the place where he can become the minister of salvation to others. The Holy Spirit will bring the worker back again and again to the stained places in memory and will make them the sweetest, the most radiant portion of that one's inner life with God. The great marvel of God's grace is that "where sin abounded, grace abounded much more."

The "Seeing" of the Disciples

"Then after three years I went up to Jerusalem to see Peter, and remained with him fifteen days" (Gal. 1:18).

Think of Paul after three years in Arabia, where he was altogether broken and then remade by the grace of God, coming to Peter and being with him for fifteen days—can you imagine what happened? How Peter would go over the whole story, beginning with the scenes on the lake right on to the Garden of Gethsemane and the cross; and Peter would take Paul to the communion service, and they would see widows there, made so by Paul. Think what a memory like that would mean to a man of acute sensitiveness. It takes great courage for a forgiven man to come in contact with those whom he has wronged. Paul was ever after concerned for the widows and orphans, remembering what he had done. It was these things that brought Paul to the place of saying, "I determined not to know anything among you except Jesus Christ and Him crucified." This element comes into our lives too. Every time the Spirit of God puts His finger on some wrong in the past and the tears of the soul commence, it is that He may show the marvel of His salvation.

Spiritual Appreciation

"Therefore, from now on, we regard no one according to the flesh. Even though we have known Christ according to the flesh, yet now we know Him thus no longer" (2 Cor. 5:16).

"From the Old Testament point of view the progress is made from the knowledge of Christ to the knowledge of Jesus; from the New Testament point of view the progress is made from the knowledge of Jesus to the knowledge of Christ" (Bengel). With us the progress is neither of these. It is from the standpoint of a personal emancipation that we begin to learn who the historic Jesus Christ was. The phrase "Back to Jesus" is right only if we go back to Jesus and know Him in the way Paul knew Him, that is, after the Spirit. ". . . who, being in the form of God"—part of the Trinity— "He humbled Himself" of that form and took on Him another form, the form of a servant. Paul knew Jesus Christ in neither of these forms; he never saw Him in the form of God, because no man has ever seen God; and he never saw Him in the days of His flesh. Paul only knew Jesus Christ after He was glorified, a unique being—God manifested in glorified flesh; consequently Paul reasons differently from the other apostles; he is the one used by the Holy Spirit to give us the doctrine of the person of Christ. We can never know Jesus "after the flesh" as the early disciples did, we know Him only after the Spirit, hence the insistence on receiving the Spirit.

Are we putting anything that Christ has done in the place of His cross? It is a snare that continually besets us until we learn the passion of Paul's life: the only thing I am determined to know among you is "Jesus Christ and Him crucified". What constitutes the call of God to preach? Not that I have a special gift, not that God has sanctified me; but that by the marvel of His grace I have caught God's meaning in the cross of Christ, and life can never be the same again. Many of us who call ourselves Christian workers ought to be learners in God's school of Calvary. It is of immense value to know what the cross of Christ can do for me, but that does not constitute a preacher: a preacher is constituted by the fact that he has seen God's heart revealed in the cross of Christ, and says, "I am determined henceforth to preach nothing but Jesus Christ and Him crucified," not—"myself crucified with Christ," that is a mere experience; but—"the one figure I am determined to present is Jesus Christ, and Him crucified."

LOYALTY TO THE FORLORN HOPE

"If I had said, 'I will speak thus,' behold, I would have been untrue to the generation of Your children" (Ps. 73:15).

Loyalty to God and to God's children is the supreme test in the life of a saint. We are never free from disloyalty unless we are actually loyal. The psalmist realized that to speak as he had been doing was to be a traitor to God's children. With whom are we standing in this generation? Are we being loyal to God and to His saints? Indignation towards every yoke but the yoke of Christ is the only attitude for the saint. Our discouragement arises from egotism. Discouragement is "disenchanted egotism"—the heart knocked out of what I want. A saint cannot be discouraged any more than Jesus Christ could be. "He will not fail nor be discouraged." Why? Because He never wanted anything but His Father's will. We become discouraged because we do not like being told the truth; we look only for those things that will quicken and enliven us.

Faith in God Reigning over the World

Psalm 73:1–14

It is easy to *say* God reigns, and then to see Satan, suffering, and sin reigning, and God apparently powerless. Belief in God must be tried before it is of value to God or to a child of His. It is the trial of our faith that makes us wealthy in God's sight. We begin by saying, "I know that God is love, that He is just and holy and true"; then we come up against common sense facts that flatly contradict what we said we believed. Are we going to succumb, as the psalmist nearly did, to pessimistic moods of intellect and say, "After all I must abandon that view of God"? If we try to answer the problems of this world by intellectual or scientific methods we shall go mad, or else deny that the problems exist. Never get into the ostrich-like attitude of Christian Science, and say that there is no such thing as death or sin or pain. Jesus Christ makes us open our eyes and look at these things. God is the only being who can stand the slander that arises because the devil and pain and sin are in the world. Stand true to the life hid with Christ in God and to the facts you have to face. You will have no answer intellectually, but your faith in God will be so unshakably firm that others will begin to see there is an answer they have never guessed. "I am the way, the truth, and the life."

Metaphysically it may be true to say that suffering is the outcome of sin, but what about the problems that theory produces? What is needed is not a solution satisfying to the mind, but a moral conception, a solution that comes through a personal relationship to God whose character we believe in but whose ways we are unable to explain as yet. We are not true to God's character today, but to our creeds, to our presentations of truth, and to our experiences; but these do not cover all the facts. The question is, will the child of God in the "in between" of this life where sin and Satan are rampant, remain true to God when everything is going contrary to what he believes God's character to be?

"For I was envious of the boastful, when I saw the prosperity of the wicked." The prosperity of the wicked remains a problem to everyone who is outside the life hid with Christ in God. It is only from that center that we come slowly by faith to a solution. The problem persists, and it cannot be answered intellectually or psychologically. Moral and spiritual integrity cannot be measured by God's blessings. God sends His favors on good and bad alike. The blessings of God are an indication that God is overflowing in grace and benediction irrespective of a man's relationship to Him. Men may partake of the blessings of God and yet never come into relationship with Him (see Matt. 5:45–48).

Faith in God Ruling among Worldliness

Psalm 73:15–22

It is concentration on God that keeps us free from moral and spiritual panic. The one message all through the Sermon on the Mount is—concentrate on God, and be carefully careless about everything else. Today we are evading concentration on God and devoting ourselves to the cause of Christian work. The busyness of duties will knock us out of relationship to God more quickly than the devil. Most of us are surrounded with Christian fellowship and live such sheltered lives that we forget there are those who have to live a life of unspotted holiness in the midst of moral abominations, and God does not take them out of it. If once we lose sight of the personal relationship to God, right and wrong become relative, not absolute. "Make allowances." Never! We can only learn by the life hid with Christ in God with what a fierce purity we must confront the horror of the world. The purity of Christ is not a winsome thing, it hurts perilously everything that is not pure. "For our God is a consuming fire." If you stand true to the purity of Christ, you will have to meet problems connected with the margins of your bodily life, and if you turn for one second in public or in secret from walking in the light as God is in the light, you will lose the distinction between absolute right and wrong and make the word "affinity" an excuse to further orders. Test every emotional affinity in this way—"If I let this thing have its way, what will it mean?" If you can see the end of it to be wrong, grip it on the threshold of your mind, and at the peril of your soul never let it encroach again upon your attention. Whenever you meet with difficulties, whether they are intellectual or circumstantial or physical, remain loyal to God. Don't compromise. If you do, everyone around you will suffer from your faithlessness, because you are disloyal to Jesus Christ and His way of looking at things. Never run away with the idea that you can ever do a thing or have an attitude of mind before God which no one else need know anything about. A man is what he is in the dark. Remain loyal to God and to His saints in private and in public, and you will find that not only are you continually with God, but that God is counting on you.

Faith in God Recognizing His Own Word

Psalm 73:23–28

God and His promises are eternal. "The gift of God is eternal life." Jesus Christ came to give us eternal life, a life in which there is neither time nor space, which cannot be marked with suffering or death; it is the life Jesus lived. Some prayers are so big, and God has such a surprising answer for us, that He keeps us waiting for the manifestation. The saint is one who knows, "Nevertheless I am continually with You," in Your presence; consequently there is no perplexity or confusion if the manifestation of the answer in a particular domain is withheld. There is no logic for faith or for suffering. The region in which God deals with us in the region of implicit life that cannot be put into words.

When we try to carry out the commands of Christ it is the Christians who say, "Don't be so stupid; don't strain human nature; do you think you are a special favorite of God's?" That is the way loyalty to God is deflected. Our minds have to remain loyal to God and to His saints, and we must crucify resolutely every impression that is contrary. If we give way to a dark mood of depression, we sin against God and His saints. The purpose of God through every experience is to make us unlearn what we bring with us until we are as simple as children before Him.

SPIRITUAL EVOLUTION

The world today is obsessed with the idea of evolution. We hear speculations about the superman, we are told we are getting better and better; but what we are tending towards we don't know. The remarkable thing about the spiritual evolution represented by Jesus Christ is that the goal is given to us at the start, namely, Jesus Christ Himself. The natural view and the Bible's view of man are different; the natural point of view is that man is a great being in the making, his achievements are a wonderful promise of what he is going to be; the Bible's point of view is that man is a magnificent ruin of what God designed him to be. The Bible does not look forward to an evolution of mankind; the Bible talks of a revolution—"You must be born again." That is not a command but the statement of a foundation fact. There must be a break in a man's life before he enters into the spiritual realm. God and man as God created him were at one, but severance came with the introduction of sin; then Jesus Christ came, and in Him God and man are again made at one. Jesus Christ did not evolve out of history, He came into history from outside history; He is not the best human being the world has ever seen, He is a being who cannot be accounted for by the human race at all. Jesus Christ is the first and the last, and Paul uses the figure of Jesus as the goal to which the whole human race is to attain—"till we all come . . . to the measure of the stature of the fullness of Christ."

Struggle for Self

"Strive to enter through the narrow gate" (Luke 13:24).

Everyone has to begin with this struggle for self, and striving to enter in at the narrow gate is a picture of the struggle. Anything that does not enter in at the narrow gate, for example, selfishness, self-interest, self-indulgence, ends in destruction. The struggle to enter in, no matter with what it may be in connection, braces us morally. Self-indulgence is a refusal to struggle, a refusal to make ourselves fit. We must be right ourselves before we can help others to be right.

If you make a moral struggle and gain a moral victory, you will be a benefit to all you come across, whereas if you do not struggle, you act as a moral pollution. Gain a moral victory in chastity or in your emotional life, it may be known to no one but yourself, and you are an untold benefit to everyone else; but if you refuse to struggle everyone else is weakened. This is a recognized psychological law, although little known. Struggle to gain the mastery over selfishness, and you will be a tremendous assistance; but if you don't overcome the tendency to spiritual sluggishness and self-indulgence, you are a hindrance to all around you. These things are intangible, but they are there, and Jesus says to us, "Strive to enter through the narrow gate." You never get through alone. If you struggle to get through, others are the stronger and better for knowing you. The men and women who lift and inspire us are those who struggle for self, not for self-assertiveness, that is a sign of weakness, but for the development of personality. There are some people in whose company you cannot have a mean thought without being instantly rebuked.

Struggle for Others

"And the second [commandment], like it, is this: 'You shall love your neighbor as yourself'" (Mark 12:31).

Whenever you touch your own true interests, others are involved at once. No man can gain a moral or spiritual victory without gaining an interest in other men. If you struggle and overcome, you will see that the other man gets a chance to fight his own moral battle too. The danger of false moral train- ing is that it does not allow a man the chance to fight for himself or for others. We are inclined to be amateur provi- dences over other lives spiritually, to so shield them that they are brought up like hothouse plants instead of being where moral victories should be gained. No man or woman ought to be innocent, a woman ought to be pure and a man ought to be virtuous. Innocence has to be transformed into purity through being brought into contact with things that are impure and overcoming them, thus establishing purity. A virtuous man or woman is a tremendous assistance wherever he or she goes.

"Greater love has no one than this, than to lay down one's life for his friends"—and Jesus says—"I have called you friends." The characteristic of your life if you are devoted to Jesus, is that you lay down your life for Him, not die for Him, but lay down your life for Him. Paul puts it—". . . our- selves your servants for Jesus' sake." You are the servant of other men for His sake. If you are devoted to the cause of humanity, you will soon be exhausted and have your heart broken by ingratitude, but if the mainspring of your service is love for Jesus, you can serve men although they treat you as a doormat. Never look for justice in this world, but never cease to give it. If you do look for justice, you cease to struggle for your true self.

Struggle for Co-relation

"Therefore be followers of God as dear children. And walk in love, as Christ also has loved us . . ." (Eph. 5:1–2).

If I struggle for myself on the right line, I struggle for others also, and the struggle establishes a co-relation between God and myself, and the characteristic of the life is a strong family likeness to Jesus. A self indwelt by Jesus becomes like Him. "Walk in love, as Christ also has loved us." Jesus has loved me to the end of all my meanness and selfishness and sin; now, He says, show that same love to others. "For if you forgive men their trespasses, your heavenly Father will also forgive you"— that is, I am to ask to be forgiven, not on the ground of the atonement, but because I forgive. "But if you do not forgive men their trespasses, neither will your Father forgive your trespasses." That is hard hitting. Am I prepared to show the man who does evil to me the love God has shown to me? I have to learn to identify myself with God's interests in other people, and God's interests are never my selfish interests, but always His interests. When the Spirit of God comes into a man, He gives him a worldwide outlook. God has no favorites, ". . . that we may present every man perfect in Christ Jesus. To this end, I also labor, striving according to His working which works in me mightily." The benefit of my life to others is in proportion to whether I am making this struggle for the self God designed me to be, and my worth to God is in proportion to my getting into co-relation with Him, getting His point of view about everything.

AT GOD'S DISCRETION

"It is the glory of God to conceal a matter" (Prov. 25:2).

This is not an isolated phrase, the idea runs all through the Bible, see Deuteronomy 29:29: "The secret things belong to the LORD our God, but those things which are revealed belong to us and to our children forever . . ."; Romans 11:33: "Oh, the depth of the riches both of the wisdom and knowledge of God! How unsearchable are His judgments and His ways past finding out!" The purpose of mystery is not to tantalize us and make us feel that we cannot comprehend; it is a generous purpose, and meant to assure us that slowly and surely as we can bear it, the full revelation of God will be made clear.

It is the glory of God to conceal His teaching in obedience: we only know as we obey. "If anyone wants to do His will, he shall know concerning the doctrine . . . ." It is only by way of obedience that we understand the teaching of God. Bring it straight down to the commonplace things: Have I done the duty that lies nearest? Have I obeyed God there? If not, I shall never fathom the mysteries of God, however much I may try. When once I obey there, I receive a revelation of the meaning of God's teaching for me. How many of us have obeyed the bit of God's truth we do know?

Experience is a gateway to understanding, not an end in itself. We can be bound in other ways than by sin; we can be bound by the limits of the very experiences that were meant to lead us into the secrets of God. The faith of many really spiritual Christians is eclipsed today, and the reason it is eclipsed is that they tried to remain true and consistent to the narrow confines of their experience instead of getting out into the light of God. God wants to get us into the place where He holds absolutely, and experiences never bother us. Oh, the relief of it! The burden gone, the effort gone, no conscious experience left, because Jesus Christ is all and in all.

God has hidden the glory of His teaching in the experience of temptation. "My brethren, count it all joy when you fall into various trials," says the apostle James. "To him who overcomes I will give some of the hidden manna." The feast is just beyond the fight; when you have been through the fight, there is the wondrous joy and triumph of the feast. We learn to thank God for the trial of our faith because it works patience. The thing that is precious in the sight of God is faith that has been tried. Tried faith is spendable; it is so much wealth stored up in heaven, and the more we go through the trial of our faith, the wealthier we become in the heavenly regions.

"Blessed are the pure in heart." If we go on obeying God, we shall find that "light is sown for the righteous." We are so impatient—"I thought God's purpose was to make me full of happiness and joy." It is, but it is happiness and joy from God's standpoint, not from ours. God always ignores the present perfection for the ultimate perfection. We bring God to the bar of our judgment and say hard things about Him—"Why does God bring thunderclouds and disasters when we want green pastures and still waters?" Bit by bit we find, behind the clouds, the Father's feet; behind the lightning, an abiding day that has no night; behind the thunder a still small voice that comforts with a comfort that is unspeakable.

It is the glory of God to conceal His treasures in embarrassments, that is, in things that involve us in difficulty. "I will give you the treasures of darkness." We would never have suspected that treasures were hidden there, and in order to get them we have to go through things that involve us in perplexity. There is nothing more wearying to the eye than perpetual sunshine, and the same is true spiritually. The valley of the shadow gives us time to reflect, and we learn to praise God for the valley because in it our soul was restored in its communion with God. God gives us a new revelation of His kindness in the valley of the shadow. What are the days and the experiences that have furthered us most? The days of green pastures, of absolute ease? No, they have their value; but the days that have furthered us most in character are the days of stress and cloud, the days when we could not see our way but had to stand still and wait; and as we waited, the comforting and sustaining and restoring of God came in a way we never imagined possible before.

God wants us to realize His sovereignty. We are apt to tie God up in His own laws and allow Him no free will. We say we know what God will do, and suddenly He upsets all our calculations by working in unprecedented ways; just when we expected He would do a certain thing, He did the opposite. There are unexpected issues in life; unexpected joys when we looked for sorrow, and sorrow when we expected joy, until we learn to say "my expectation is from Him." (Psalm 62:5).

Again, God disciplines us by disappointment. Life may have been going on like a torrent, then suddenly down comes a barrier of disappointment, until slowly we learn that the disappointment was His appointment. God hides His treasures in darkness, and many a radiant star that was not seen before comes out. In some lives you can see the treasure, there is a sweetness and beauty about them, "the incorruptible ornament of a gentle and quiet spirit," and you wonder where the winsome power of God came from. It came from the dark places where God revealed His sovereign will in unexpected issues. "You have relieved me when I was in distress."

"It is the glory of God to conceal a matter." God will not have us come with an impatient curiosity. Moral or intellectual or spiritual insanity must result if we push down barriers which God has placed before our spiritual progress is fit for the revelation. This is a day of intolerant inquisitiveness. Men will not wait for the slow, steady, majestic way of the Son of God; they try to enter in by this door and that door. "But one of the elders said to me, 'Do not weep. Behold, the Lion of the tribe of Judah, the Root of David, has prevailed to open the scroll and to loose its seven seals' " (Rev. 5:5). The barriers are placed by a holy God, and He has told us clearly—"Not that way." God grant we may accept His clouds and mysteries, and be led into His inner secrets by obedient trust.

CELEBRATION OR SURRENDER?

"But God forbid that I should glory except in the cross of our Lord Jesus Christ, by whom the world has been crucified to me, and I to the world" (Gal. 6:14).

We are much more ready to celebrate what Jesus Christ has done than to surrender to Him. I do not mean the initial surrender to God of a sinner, but the more glorious surrender to God of a saint.

Triviality—or, taken up with externals

Paul is writing to really spiritual people, but they were being made the center of a conflict of rival paths to perfection. He says, in effect, "When I 'placarded' Christ crucified before you, you were fascinated at once; now others are 'placarding' ritual and laws, and you are heeding them." If rites and ceremonies are put as a road to perfection they will become the path away from it. To put prayer, devotion, obedience, con-secration, or any experience, as the means of sanctification is the proof that we are on the wrong line. In sanctification the one reality is the Lord Himself; if you know Him, you will pay no attention to experiences. Experiences are only a doorway to lead us into the awe and wonder of the revelation of God. Let experiences come and go; bank on the Lord.

The Galatians were relapsing not into sin, but into fixity; they had the jargon of sanctimoniousness, but no real vigorous life. It is easy to think that we are to be specimens of what God can do. According to the New Testament, a saint is a piece of rugged human stuff remade by the atonement into oneness with God by the power of the Holy Spirit. The tendency to stereotype Christian experience is an abiding danger; it leads to the amateur providence attitude—"I am not likely to go wrong, but you are." I become, as it were, god almighty over a particular doctrine and imagine that everyone else is off on a side track. For example, when I think I can define what sanctification is, I have done something God refuses to do. Books about sanctification are much clearer than the Bible. The Bible is uncommonly confusing, so is human life. There is only one thing that is simple, and that is our relationship to Jesus Christ. What is needed today is not so much a revival as a resurgent form of awakening, the incoming of the tremendous life of God in a new form.

The cure for triviality spiritually is a new note of greatness born of the realization of what it cost Jesus Christ to produce His salvation in us. Only when we continually face the cross are we safe from the danger of triviality and internal hypocrisy. Today the clamor is "do"; but the great need is to face our souls with God until the sterling stamp and testimony of the life is—"But God forbid that I should glory except in the cross of our Lord Jesus Christ." We are so taken up with actual happenings that we forget the one fundamental thing, namely, the cross. Beware of any fascination that takes you away from the center.

Temporariness—or, uncertainty of foundations

Paul was alarmed over these Galatian Christians because they were losing the foundation setting. He says, "I am afraid for you . . ." (4:9–11). The reason for temporariness is because we will not think. It is much easier not to think, much more peaceful. A devotee to doctrines does not need to think, but a man who is devoted to Jesus Christ is obliged to think, and to think every day of his life, and he must allow nothing to dissipate his thinking. It is not courage men lack, but concentration on Jesus Christ. We have to get out of our laziness and indifference and excuses, and rouse ourselves up to face the cross of Christ.

The cure for uncertainty is a new note of intercessory prayer. The reason for perplexity in meeting the actual occurrences of life is because we are losing face-to-face contact with Jesus Christ through His cross. We must get back to the place where we are concerned only about facing our own inner souls with Jesus Christ who searches us right down to the inmost recesses. If we will face the tremendous moral earnestness at the back of the cross, a new note will be struck in the life which will work the wonders Jesus said it would. "Whatever you ask in My name, that I will do" (John 14:13). Prayer prevails with God for men and with men for God. Can I by the passion of my prayer, pierce the darkness of a soul and give the Holy Spirit a chance to work, or do I sit mourning on the outskirts as though God had no more power than I have to lift that life? The passionate note of intercession is born in the secret places before God. Salvation is so wonderful, so full of ease and power, because of what it cost Jesus Christ. How much of the tremendous generating power of prayer that is born at the foot of the cross are those of us who recognize the eternal realities behind the actual happenings of life, putting in for others?

Toughness—or, spiritual self-satisfaction

We are so happy, so sure and so satisfied, that we have lost altogether the note of surrender which marked the life of Jesus. He sacrificed His holy self to His Father, "for their sakes I sanctify Myself"; and we have the same privilege of sacrificing ourselves to Him. Jesus Christ submitted His intelligence to the word and will of His Father; are we submitting our intelligence to Jesus Christ, or are we being caught up on the line of spiritual insubordination? False revivals come along this line. Insubordination means we will not submit our impulses and intuitions and all the forces of the inner life to Jesus Christ; we will not turn to see the voice that speaks. "Then I turned to see the voice that spoke with me" (Rev. 1:12). Will is the whole man active, and the whole active power and force of the saint is to be laid at the feet of Jesus Christ. We busy ourselves with work for Him while He waits for all our individual energy to be curbed and submitted to Him that He may redirect it into the channels He wants. "He who believes in Me, . . . out of his heart will flow rivers of living water."

Are we more anxious to be winsome to men and women than to be loyal to God? More anxious to be friends of men than friends of God? More anxious to sympathize with men and women who are wrong than to sympathize with God? Are we getting unstable on the foundation truths of the redemption? Beware lest it be said of us that we are "enemies of the cross of Christ." May the great note of our lives be—"In the cross of Christ I glory"; no more feeble celebrations, but the great note of surrender, "I am not my own; I am bought at a price." Keep that sterling note in front of your soul, in front of your heart and mind. In Christ's name, what do we know about the craving for Jesus Christ's honor, the tremendous heart hunger and passion of a man like the apostle Paul—"I could wish that I myself were accursed from Christ for my brethren"? The servant of Jesus Christ has no private history other than his private history with his Lord.

"What is wanted is the restatement of our creeds." No, what is wanted is to be brought face to face with the one abiding reality, God Himself; to know that only through the cross, and the efficacy of the Holy Spirit at work through the cross, can men be lifted up. The test of Jesus Christ's salvation is that it produces Christlikeness, a life of absolute simplicity before God. Let us be what will satisfy His heart.

THE SACRAMENT OF SILENCE

"My soul, wait silently for God alone" (Ps. 62:5).

A great deal of silence arises from sullenness or from exhaustion, but the silence the psalmist is alluding to is the silence which springs from the absolute certainty that God knows what He is doing. The psalmist is determined to break up the drowsiness of his own soul and to bring himself into a watchfulness before God. Silent prayer is, in reality, concentration on God. You say, "But it is not easy to concentrate on God"; it is just because it is not easy that so few learn the secret of doing it. We need to rouse ourselves up out of our indifference, out of drifting into mere jabbering before God, and get into an attitude of fruitful vigilance. Is silent prayer to us an experience of waiting upon God, or is it a "cotton wool" experience? utterly dim and dark? a time which we simply endure until it is over? If you want discerning vision about anything, you have to make an effort and call in your wandering attention. Mental wool-gathering can be stopped if the will is roused. Prayer is an effort of will, and the great battle in prayer is the overcoming of mental wool-gathering. We put things down to the devil when we should put them down to our own inability to concentrate. "My soul, wait silently for

God alone," that is, "pull yourself together and be silent before God."

"MY SOUL, wait silently for God alone."

Soul is my personal spirit as it reasons, and thinks, and looks at things; I have to call my powers together and concentrate on God. It is possible to concentrate and yet not concentrate on God. We may have a dead set about our lives, but it may be a dead set on comfort or on money, not a dead set on God and on the wonder and majesty of His dealings. The rich fool in our Lord's parable did not ask his soul to consider God, but to consider his possessions—"Soul, you have many goods laid up for many years; take your ease; eat, drink, and be merry." Be careful to concentrate on a worthy object. "Wait silently for God alone." Stop all false hurry and spend time in communion with God. Think of the benediction which comes to your disposition by waiting upon God! Some of us are in such a hurry that we distort God's blessings for ourselves and for others. "Wait silently on God alone"; to do that will demand at the beginning the severest mental effort we have ever put forth.

To be "silent before God" does not mean drifting into mere feeling, or sinking into reverie, but deliberately getting into the center of things and focusing on God. When you have been brought into relationship with God through the atonement of the Lord Jesus Christ and are concentrating on Him, you will experience wonderful times of communion. As you wait only upon God, concentrating on the glorious outlines of His salva⟨tion, there will come into you the steeping peace of God, the certainty that you are in the place where God is doing all in accordance with His will. In this earnest life of communion with God, the stress of the life is in the right place, that is, you are not in earnest in order that God may recognize you as His child; your earnestness is the outcome of real communion with God.

"My soul, WAIT silently for God alone."

To wait upon God is not to sit with folded hands and do nothing, but to wait as men who wait for the harvest. The farmer does not wait idly but with intense activity, he keeps industriously "at it" until the harvest. To wait upon God is the perfection of activity. We are told to "rest in the LORD," not to rust. We talk of resting in the Lord but it is often only a pious expression; in the Bible, resting in the Lord is the patience of godly confidence. "In returning and rest you shall be saved . . . . And you said, 'No, for we will flee on horses,'" that is, we will take the initiative. When we take the initiative we put our wits on the throne, we do not worship God. God never guides His children by their own initiative. The only initiative we have to take is the initiative of worshiping God.

"For my expectation is from Him." Watch the moon as it shines across the sea; there is a silver pathway of light across the billows straight from the distant horizon to the shore, a line of communication over everything between. If you are God's child, there is this expectant line of communication always between you and God. Your experience may be a dreary wilderness, a sea of despair, a dusty, sandy waste with no shade—but over all is a line of communication between you and God. "A highway shall be there, and a road." Or yours may be the experience of having to walk at the bottom of the sea—"All Your billows and Your waves passed over me," yet, "When you pass through the waters, I will be with you." Or it may be the extraordinarily consuming difficulties that make up the burden of life—is there a line of communication there? "The mountains melt like wax at the presence of the LORD." "My expectation is from Him." Have we learned this sacrament of silence, this secret of inner communion with God?

"He only is my rock." A rock conveys the idea of an encircling guard, as that of a mother watching her child who is learning to walk; should the child fall, he falls into the encircling love and watchfulness of the mother's care. "The LORD is my rock," my encircling guard. Where did the psalmist learn this truth? In the school of silent waiting upon God. The Rock of Ages is the great sheltering encirclement; we are watched over by the mother-guardianship of God. "I am el-Shaddai," the father-mother God. "He is my strong tower [fortress] and my defense." The Lord Himself is our inviolable place of safety. There is a loftiness and an inaccessibility about the heavenly places in Christ Jesus. The higher you climb the purer the air until you come to the place where the least microbe is unable to live, and spiritually there is an inaccessible place of absolute security. "You have set Your house of defense [fortress] very high."

"I shall not be greatly moved." God lifts us up and poises us in Himself as surely as He has established the stars.

"My soul, wait silently for God alone." Rouse your soul out of its drowsiness to consider God. Fix your attention on God, on the great themes of His redemption and His holiness, on the great and glorious outlines of His character, be silent to Him there; then be as busy as you like in the ordinary affairs of life. Be like the Lord Jesus; when He was sound asleep in the fishing boat, He knew that His Father would waken Him when he wanted Him. This is a marvelous picture of confidence in God.

"My soul, wait silently for God alone."

SPIRITUAL CONFUSION

"You do not know what you ask" (Matt. 20:22).

At times in spiritual life there is confusion, and the usual way out is to say there ought to be no confusion. Some of us are inclined to be fanatical; we won't pay any attention to things that are not black or white, right or wrong. There are very few things that are black or white, right or wrong, and until we recognize this we are apt to be insolent or indifferent towards anything in between. A fog is as real as clear sunshine; if we don't pay any attention to the fog, we shall come to disaster. There are things in the spiritual life which are confused, not because we have disobeyed, but owing to the very nature of things. The confusion arises from being unschooled spiritually.

The Shrouding of His Friendship

Luke 11:5–8

"And he will answer from within and say, 'Do not trouble me; the door is now shut . . .'" (v. 7).

There is a time in spiritual life when God does not seem to be a friend. Everything was clear and easily marked and understood for a while, but now we find ourselves in a condition of darkness and desolation. The parable of the persistent friend is the illustration Jesus gives of how the heavenly Father will appear in times of spiritual confusion—as a man who does not care for his friends. We are in need, or our friends or our families are in need, and though we go to God who has been our friend all through, He does nothing at all. It is as if Jesus said to His disciples, "There are times when the heavenly Father will look like that, but don't give up, remember I have told you, 'Everyone who asks receives.'" In the meantime the friendship of God is completely shrouded. There are things that have no explanation, but maintain your relationship to God, "hang in" in confidence in Him, and the time will come when everything will be explained. It is only by going through the confusion that we shall get at what God wants us to get at.

Never say God has done what He has not done because it sounds better to say it; never pretend to have an answer when you have not. Jesus said, "Everyone who asks receives." We say, "I have asked but I have not received." It is because we ask in spiritual confusion. Jesus said to James and John: "You do not know what you ask"; they were brought into fellowship with Jesus Christ's cup and baptism, but not in the way they expected.

The Shadow on His Fatherhood

Luke 11:11–12

"If a son asks for bread from any father among you, will he give him a stone?" (v. 11).

Jesus says there are times when our heavenly Father will appear as if He were a most unnatural father, callous and indifferent—I asked for bread and He gave me a stone, and there is a shadow on His fatherhood. But remember that Jesus told us, "Everyone who asks receives." When we get into spiritual confusion the usual way out is to say we have made a blunder, and we go back instead of forward. "I don't know what to do; I am up against a stone wall." Will you "hang in" to what Jesus said? If there is a shadow on the face of the fatherhood of God just now, remain confident that ultimately He will give His clear issue as Jesus said. It is not a question of black or white, right or wrong, or being in communion or out of communion, but a question of God taking us by a way which in the meantime we do not understand.

The Strangeness of His Faithfulness

Luke 18:1–8

"And shall God not avenge His own elect who cry out day and night to Him, though He bears long with them?" (v. 7).

There are times when the heavenly Father will look as if He were an unjust judge. But remember that Jesus says that He is not. In the meantime there is a cloud on the friendship of the heart, and even love itself has to wait often in pain and tears for the blessing of fuller communion. The time is coming when we shall see perfectly clearly, but it is only through confusion that we can get to a clear outline.

State definitely to yourself the things that are confused; note the things that are not clear black and white. There are no problems at all over right and wrong. Human life is not made up of right and wrong, but of things which are not quite clear—"I do not know what God would have me do in this matter." Resolve in faith that what Jesus said is true, "Every-one who asks receives." And in the meantime do the duty that lies nearest, waiting and watching. If the friendship of God is shrouded and it looks as if He is not going to do any-thing, then remain dumb. The real problems are very heavy. Instead of God being a father loving and kind, it looks at times as if He were totally indifferent. Remember, God has bigger issues at stake on the ground of His redemption than the particular setting in which we ask. In the meantime we do not know what God is doing, but we are certain that what Jesus says is true. "If you then, being evil, know how to give good gifts to your children, how much more will your heavenly Father give the Holy Spirit to those who ask Him!" And when we are the possessors of the Holy Spirit we shall justify God all through.

Until we have been disciplined properly by means of spiritual confusion we shall always want to bank on God's miracles and refuse to do the moral thing ourselves. It is much easier to ask God to do our work for us than to do it ourselves—"Oh well, I will pray and ask God to clean this thing up for me." God won't. We must do our own work. Prayer is always a temptation to bank on a miracle instead of a moral issue until we are disciplined. God will do more than we can do, but only in relationship to our spiritual growth. When we have received the gift of the Holy Spirit, we have to learn to obey God in every detail, then the shroudings will be lifted, the shadows will disappear, the strangeness will go, and we shall begin to understand the friendship and the fatherhood and the faithfulness of God with regard to our lives.

"Nevertheless, when the Son of Man comes, will He really find faith on the earth?" Will He find the faith that banks on Him in spite of the confusion?

THE LONG TRAIL TO SPIRITUAL REALITY

"But now we do not yet see all things put under Him" (Heb. 2:8).

When we are busy with our own outlook on life, it seems as if God were indifferent. Our human patience, as well as our impatience, gets to the point of saying, "Why does not God do things?" Redemption is complete; we believe that our Lord has all power in heaven and on earth, then why is it such a long while before things happen? Why is God so long in making actual His answers to our prayers? When in such a state of mind we are capable of becoming bitter against God unless we are led into the inner secret of our Lord's own attitude.

The Vision of the Long Way

Matt. 4:1.

For thirty years Jesus had remained unknown, then He was baptized and had a wonderful manifestation of the Father's approval, and the next thing we read is that He is "led up by the Spirit into the wilderness to be tempted by the devil." The same thing puzzles us in our own spiritual experience; we have been born from above. We have had the baptism of the Holy Spirit—surely we are fit now to do something for God; and God deliberately puts us on the shelf, amongst the dust and the cobwebs, in an utterly unaccountable way.

The agony Jesus went through in the temptation was surely because He had the vision of the long way and saw the suffering it would entail on men through all the ages if He took His Father's way. He knew it in a way we cannot conceive. His sensitiveness is beyond anything we can imagine. If He had not been true to His Father's way, His own home would not have been upset, His own nation would not have blasphemed the Holy Spirit. The way to approach Gethsemane is to try to understand the temptation.

Each of the temptations presented to our Lord by Satan had this as its center: "You will get the kingship of men and the saviorhood of the world if You will take a 'shortcut'—put man's needs first, and he will crown You king; do something extraordinarily wonderful, indicative of Your power, and man will crown You king; compromise with evil, and You will get the kingship of men." Jesus could have brought the whole thing about suddenly (cf. John 6:15); but He did not. He withstood Satan and took the stupendously long way.

When we obey Jesus Christ it is never a question of what it costs us—it does not cost us anything, it is a delight—but of what it costs those whom we love, and there is always the danger of yielding to the temptation of the "shortcut." Am I prepared to let my obedience to God cost other people something? Jesus deliberately took the long trail, and He says, "a disciple is not above his teacher." "Because you have kept My command to persevere . . . ." We want to hurry things up by revivals. Over and over again we take the devil's advice and say, "It must be done quickly—the need is the call; men must be saved." An understanding of the inwardness of our Lord's temptation will throw light on the progress of Christian history as well as on personal experience.

Why does God take such a long time? Because of what He is after, namely, "bringing many sons to glory." It takes time to make a son. We are not made sons of God by magic; we are saved in the great supernatural sense by the sovereign work of God's grace, but sonship is a different matter. I have to become a son of God by deliberate discernment and understanding and chastisement, not by spiritual necromancy, imagining I can ascend to heaven in leaps and bounds. The "shortcut" would make men mechanisms, not sons, with no discernment of God. If God did not shield His only begotten Son from any of the requirements of sonship ("though He was a Son, yet He learned obedience by the things which He suffered," (Heb. 5:8), He will not shield us from all the requirements of being His sons and daughters by adoption.

The Valley of the Long Wait

"For I consider that the sufferings of this present time are not worthy to be compared with the glory which shall be revealed in us" (Rom. 8:18).

It is a long wait until the sons of God appear, and they only appear by the deliberate simplicity of obedience to Him. When the Spirit of God comes into a man the first thing that happens is the corruption of the natural virtues. Natural virtues are remnants of the human race as God designed it; when a man is born again his natural virtues begin to crumble, and he is plunged into perplexity. Natural good has to die in me before the best can come. That is the keynote of spiritual reality. It is not the bad that is the enemy of God, but the good that is not good enough. We say that sin is the enemy of God—sin is *our* enemy. The enemy of God in me is morality based on a denial of Jesus, that is, the rectitude that is not based on spiritual regeneration.

The Voice of the Living Worship

John 14:6

Jesus does not take men and say, "This is the truth and if you don't believe it you will be damned." He simply shows us the truth—"I am the . . . truth," and leaves us alone. We name His name, but is He the truth to us in our bodily life, in our common sense life, in our intellectual and emotional life? It takes a long while for us to begin to see that Jesus Christ is the truth. Truths exist that have no meaning for us until we get into the domain of their power, "Most assuredly, I say to you, unless one is born again, he cannot see the kingdom of God" (John 3:3). We want to get at truth by "shortcuts"; the wonder is our Lord's amazing patience. He never insists that we take His way; He simply says, "I am the way." We might as well learn to take His way at the beginning, but we won't, we are determined on our own way. Do I believe that God can only come to other men in the way He comes to me?

"Unless you . . . become as little children . . . ." We won't become as little children, we have notions of our own, somewhere within us all is the "superior person." There is nothing simpler or more exquisite than a little child, and Jesus says you must become like that. We say, "But I am so-and-so, and I have had these experiences, and I have ideas of my own." Or we may not say it, but we think it. It takes a long time to realize what Jesus is after, and the person you need most patience with is yourself. God takes deliberate time with us, He does not hurry, because we can only appreciate His point of view by a long discipline. The grace of God abides always the same. By His grace we stand on the basis of His redemption; but we ought to be making headway in the development of our personal sonship.

AUTOBIOGRAPHY OF COMMUNION WITH GOD

". . . and after the earthquake a fire, but the LORD was not in the fire; and after the fire a still small voice" (1 Kings 19:12).

What is mirrored in the unique, solitary figure of Elijah is not something we all experience, although it explains what we experience. An expositor must deal with exceptional cases, but we blunder if we look in our own experience for the exceptional and sensational. There are ways in our lives about which we cannot be articulate, they go beyond our exact expression, we do not know why we are moved as we are; the explanation for it is not to be found in ourselves but in the experience of some greater soul. If we study Elijah in this experience of gloom and isolation, we shall find a line of understanding for ourselves.

Interior desolation serves a vital purpose in the life of a Christian. At the beginning of the spiritual life the consciousness of God is so wonderful that we are apt to imagine our communion with God depends upon our being conscious of His presence. Then when God begins to withdraw us into Himself, and things become mysterious, we lose our faith and get into the dark, and say, "I must have backslidden," and yet we know we have not, all we know is that we have lost our consciousness of God's presence. Madame Guyon, in commenting on her own experience, puts it thus, "To complete my distress I seemed to be left without God Himself who alone could support me in such a distressing state." "The misfortune," she adds, "is that people wish to direct God instead of resigning themselves to be directed by Him." Out of this experience of desolation, Madame Guyon learned this truth, that our faith must be built on the reality of being taken up into God's consciousness in Christ, not on our taking God into our consciousness. This means entering into a relationship with God whereby our will becomes one with the will of God. To the thought of the saints God is never far enough away to think about them, there is no separation; He thinks them. How we get there, I cannot tell you, but it is by the processes of God's training.

Conception of the Instruments of God

1 Kings 19:11

Elijah took his own initiative in telling Ahab "there shall not be dew nor rain these years, except at my word" (17:1), and during the drought God made him go up and down the land and see the havoc that drought brought about. Now, when Elijah is isolated and spiritually baffled, God brings before him in miniature a great and strong wind, an earthquake, and fire, as much as to say that these had been used as His instruments, "but the LORD was not in the wind." Elijah's conception undoubtedly was that God was in them, but he had to learn that God was not there.

Today there are colossal forces abroad and God is using them as His instruments, but He is not "in" them, that is, they are not God. It is a misconception to imagine that God is bound up in His instruments; He uses forces and powers for

His own ends, but they must never be mistaken for Himself. An instrument conveys God's message, and a man used by God ought to be a holy man: but it does not always follow that he is (cf. Matt. 7:21–22).

Conscientious Introspection before God

". . . he arose and ran for his life" (see 1 Kings 19:3–4, 10, 14).

Elijah did an actually cowardly thing, yet he was not a coward. He ran away because he was absolutely baffled, he could not understand what God was doing. We cannot judge men by what they actually do, because the reasons of two men who do the same thing may be entirely different. Another man might have run away because he was a craven coward. Elijah fled because it seemed as if he had been let down by God in everything in which he had stood for Him. "Why is my pain perpetual, and my wound incurable, which refuses to be healed? Will You surely be to me like an unreliable stream, as waters that fail [cannot be trusted]?" (Jer. 15:18). This sense of being baffled knocks everything out; a man is like a sparrow in a gale. It is not a question of losing his wits, but of realizing that he has none. The battle in spiritual life is, on whom or on what am I building my confidence?

The striking thing about Job in his experience of being baffled was that he was strictly true to what he knew; he stuck to it all through—"I will not accept a credal statement of God that denies the facts I know." Job would not tell a lie for the honor of God; neither would Elijah. "I have been very zealous for the LORD God of hosts . . . . I alone am left; and they seek to take my life." In other words, "I have spent everything for Your honor, expecting You to see me through, and now I am the only one left, and I don't want the only one left standing for You to be crushed out." Elijah was conscientious before God; his baffling went deeper than discouragement, which is "disenchanted egotism." He feared that God had failed; that He had taken on too much. The greatest fear a man has is that his hero will not get through; fear for himself is child's play. Is God going to get through? Is everything going to prove a "washout"? Is my faith in God nonsense? Can Jesus Christ do what He said He could?

Consciousness of Instruction by God

1 Kings 19:5, 7, 9, 12–13, 18

The angel did not give Elijah a vision, or explain the Scriptures to him, or do anything remarkable; he told Elijah to do the most ordinary thing, namely, "Arise and eat." The ministrations of God come over and over again in the most commonplace manner possible. We look for some great big alteration, something marvelous like the wind, or an earthquake, or fire; and the voice of God tells us to do what the most ordinary voice we know might tell us to do. "And after the fire a still small voice"—that is, "a sound of gentle stillness"—the one thing the Lord was in. Then came the command, "Go, return . . . ." God sent Elijah right back, after giving him an extraordinary heartening, to do what He had told him. The haphazard may tumble about as it likes now; Elijah has learned that God's order comes that way.

The experience of being baffled is common to us all, and the more religious and thoughtful a man is, the more intensely is he baffled. With regard to your own baffling, recognize it and state it, but don't state it dishonestly to yourself. Don't say you are not baffled if you are, and don't tell a lie in order to justify your belief in God. If you are in the dark, don't take refuge in any subterfuge which you know is not true. Never take an answer that satisfies your mind only; insist on an answer that satisfies more than your mind, an answer that satisfies by the "sound of gentle stillness." Jesus describes it as "My peace," the witness of God that goes all through you and produces a complete calm within. The first thing to do is the most obvious commonsense thing possible, the thing that is absolutely natural. When God has produced the "sound of gentle stillness" in your spirit, you will hear Him speak. "Whatever I tell you in the dark, speak in the light." Then with renewed strength you go and do the thing God had already told you to do, but with the realization that you are backed by God.

IS HE YOUR MASTER?

"You call Me Teacher and Lord, and you say well, for so I am" (John 13:13).

The most remarkable thing about the mastership of Jesus Christ is that He never insists on being master. We often feel that if only He would insist, we would obey Him. Obedience to Jesus Christ is essential, but never compulsory; He will never take means to make me obey Him. Jesus Christ will always make up for my deficiencies, He always forgives my disobedience; but if I am going to be a disciple, it is essential for me to obey Him. In the early stages we have the notion that the Christian life is one of freedom, and so it is; but freedom for one thing only—freedom to obey our master.

The Great Conception

"You call Me Teacher and Lord."

We must have our Christian conception right, and this is the right conception, that Jesus Christ is our master. We do not give enough time to brooding on this conception of our Lord; we do not do enough at it. An artist or a musician must know how to brood on his conception. It is no use being the home of furtive ideas and having conceptions that come float-ing through like sunrise clouds. The artist has to go after the idea and stick to it until it is wrought into the character of his conception. It is not easy to maintain the conception of Jesus Christ as master. Spiritual concentration is needed to do it.

The conception of mastership which we get from our natural life is totally different from the mastership of Jesus Christ, because He never insists on our obedience. He simply says, "If you love Me, keep My commandments." That is the end of it. If I do not keep His commandments, He does not come and tell me I have done the wrong thing, I know it, there is no getting away from it. If once I have been indwelt by the Holy Spirit, He will always discern that I have done the fundamentally wrong thing when I disobey Jesus Christ. Let me disobey Him, and I am the most miserable wretch out of hell. He never punishes, yet I know that His consciousness of Himself is right, that He is master.

When we are born from above and have the Holy Spirit within, He delights to glow on the Lord Jesus Christ until His features are transfigured for us. Natural love does not grow if we do not do anything at it. It is the most ordinary business to fall in love; it is the most extraordinary business to abide there. The same thing is true with regard to the love of our Lord. The Holy Spirit gives us the great power to love Jesus Christ. That is not a rare experience at all; the rare experience is to get into the conception of loving Him in such a way that the whole heart and mind and soul are taken up with Him. This experience is symbolized in Mary of Bethany when she sat at the feet of Jesus. We have to sit at His feet in disposition. A thousand and one things crowd into our everyday lives; do we bring them into this conception of Jesus as master, or have we forgotten His counsel and called ourselves master in these details? We have the conception of Him as master with regard to a prayer meeting, but we have not the conception of Him as master over our tongues, over our fingers, over our possessions, over everything that belongs to us. We call ourselves master in those domains, that is, we have the conception that we are responsible for them. As saints we are responsible for one thing only, that is, to maintain our conception right in relationship to God; this is the whole secret of the devotional life of a saint. The right conception is not Christian duty or service to men, but keeping Jesus as master. How much time do I give to brooding on the conception that makes me call Him master?

The Great Certainty

"And you say well."

At the beginning of the human race the conception was that Adam was to be master over everything but himself. He was to have dominion over the life on the earth and in the air and in the sea, but he was not to have dominion over himself, God was to have dominion over him. The temptation came on this line, in effect, "Disobey, and you will become as God." Man took dominion over himself and thereby lost his lordship over everything else. According to the Bible, the disposition of sin is my claim to my right to myself.

"A disciple is not above his teacher." The life of our Lord is our pattern, not a good man, and the one characteristic of our Lord's human life was that He was not His own master. He said, in effect, "I do not speak from My right to Myself, I speak what My Father tells Me to speak. I do not work from Myself, I work the works of My Father. I do not maintain My right to Myself, I sanctify Myself to God's holy purposes." The New Testament describes how our Lord was perfected as a human being for redemptive purposes, "though He was a Son, yet He learned obedience by the things which He suffered" (Heb. 5:8), and if I am a disciple of Jesus Christ, the great certainty is that I have to be perfected as my master, and not think it strange concerning the things God puts me through.

The Great Consciousness

" . . . for so I am."

We are apt to end where we begin, that is, in our own consciousness. Christianity is not my consciousness of God, but God's consciousness of me. We must build our faith on the reality that we are taken up into God's consciousness in Christ, not that we take God into our consciousness. This is the meaning of our Lord's counsel "consider the lilies," and it is also the explanation of the inordinate desire for manifestly successful Christian work. The great consciousness in our Lord's mind is that He is man's master, and we have to get into His consciousness. The wonderful thing about our Lord is that He will not master us. He becomes the dust under our feet. He becomes less than the breath we breathe. He becomes someone we can jeer at and utilize, someone we can do anything we like with; yet all the time He is master. We can crucify Him, we can spit on Him, we can slander Him, we can ignore Him, we can hurt Him; yet He is master. And when He shows Himself at the end of the dispensation, every man will recognize Him as master, and those who have done the cruel things to Him will be so appalled at the revelation that they will call on the rocks to cover them, and the rocks in that day will reveal that they and the earth belong to their master.

Is He your master? This is the true and lasting and eternal conception, and to have it will produce confusion in every other conception of Jesus. I am not a devotee of any cause, or an advocate of any creed; I am His. "You are not your own." I must beware of the tendency to become dissipated in my conception by false notions of Christian work, or by ideas as to what I ought to be doing. I ought to be nothing but a disciple of Jesus Christ; He will be doing through me all the time. Jesus Christ's consciousness being what it is, namely, that He is master, if I am rightly related to God and walking in the light, no matter what happens to me, it is His lookout not mine. I have simply to abandon to Him and smilingly wash my hands of the consequences. He will engineer my circumstances, He will dump me down where He chooses, He will give me money or give me none, as He likes; all I have to do is to keep my soul carefully in the conception of Him as master, "For we do not preach ourselves, but Christ Jesus the Lord, and ourselves your servants for Jesus' sake."

WHY ARE WE NOT TOLD PLAINLY?

". . . He commanded them that they should tell no one the things they had seen, till the Son of Man had risen from the dead" (Mark 9:9).

Because of the Unbearable Things

"I still have many things to say to you, but you cannot bear them now" (John 16:12).

Our Lord does not hide things from us, but they are un-bearable until we are in a fit condition of spiritual life to receive them; then the word our Lord has spoken becomes so plain that we are amazed we did not understand it before. We could not understand it before because we were not in the place either in disposition or in will where it could be borne. There must be communion with the resurrection life of Jesus before a particular word can be borne by us. "Tell the vision to no one until the Son of Man is risen from the dead" in you— until the life of the risen Christ so dominates you that you understand what the historic Christ taught.

Obtuseness is valuable sometimes. It is of God's infinite mercy that we do not understand what He says until we are in a fit condition. If God came down with His light and power, we should be witless; but our Lord never enthralls us. Satan tempted Jesus to use the power of enthrallment, and false methods of service are built up on that line. When we first know the Lord we are always tempted by the "show business," our prayers are really dictation to God. God will take us out of the obtuse stage as soon as we let the resurrection life of Jesus have its way with us.

Do we know anything about the impartation of the risen life of Jesus Christ? The evidence that we do is that His words are becoming interpretable to us. God cannot reveal anything to us if we have not His Spirit. If we have made up our minds about a doctrine, we cannot get any more light from God about it, light will never come to us on that line. An obstinate out- look will effectually hinder God's revealing anything to us. It is not sin, but unenlightenment caused by the absence of the resurrection life of Jesus.

Because of the Unbelievable Things

"His disciples said to Him, . . . 'By this we believe . . . .' Jesus answered them, 'Do you now believe?'" (John 16:29– 31).

We need to rely much deeper down consciously on the resurrection life of Jesus; to get into the habit of steadily refer- ring everything back to Him. Instead of that, we make our common sense decisions and say we hope God will bless them. He cannot—they are not in His domain. "But if I do my duty, I shan't go astray." You will; it is unbelievable, but true. You will go wrong, because you have put something that can be stated in abstract form on the throne instead of our Lord. As God's children we are never told to walk in the light of con- science or of a sense of duty; we are told to walk in the light of the Lord. When we do things from a sense of duty, we can

back it up by argument; but when we do things out of obedience to the Lord there is no logical argument possible. That
is why a saint can easily be ridiculed.

"Tell no one . . . till the Son of Man had risen from the
dead." Is Jesus Christ risen in us? Is He getting His way?
When we look back on the choice of our life work, or of our
friends, or of what we call our duty, is He really the dominating one? We can soon know whether He is. We say, "Now . . .
we believe . . ." and Jesus says, "Do you now believe? Indeed,
the hour is coming . . . that you . . . will leave Me alone."
Many a Christian worker has left his Lord alone and gone into
work from a sense of duty woven out of a need, or of a call
arising from his own particular discernment. There is no sin in
it, and no punishment attached, but when that one realizes
that he has hindered his understanding of what Jesus says and
produced for himself perplexities and sorrows, it is with shame
and contrition he has to come back like a little child and ask
the Lord to teach him all over again. "Unless you . . . become
as little children." When we do a thing from a sense of duty,
we become amateur providences and the child attitude is gone;
the power of the resurrection life of Jesus is not there. We
have put up a standard in competition with our Lord, and have
got out of contact with Him by leaning to our own understanding.

"Tell the vision to no one . . . ." So many do tell, they tell
what they saw on the mount and testify to it, but the actual
life does not tally with the vision; the Son of Man is not yet
risen in them. The words sound all right, but He is not there.
There is no communication of His life through the words, no
illumination or understanding given to seeking souls, because
the Son of Man is not yet risen in them. I wonder when He is
going to be formed in us? "My little children, for whom I labor
in birth again until Christ is formed in you" (Gal. 4:19). When

are we going to believe that unbelievable thing, that we will leave Him alone, in spite of all we say?

Because of the Unquestioned Things

". . . the time is coming when I . . . will tell you plainly about the Father" (John 16:25).

"And in that day you will ask Me nothing" (John 16:23).

When is "that day"? When the resurrection life of the Lord Jesus is the portion of our life. In that day we shall be one with the Father as Jesus said we should be, because the Holy Spirit has brought us there. No one can receive the Holy Spirit unless he is convinced of his own poverty. When we receive the Holy Spirit, He imparts the risen life of Jesus and there is no distance between the Father and His child. Have we come to this unquestioning place where there is no more perplexity of heart in regard to God? Any number of things may be dark and unexplained, but they do not come in between the heart and God. "In that day you will ask Me nothing"—you do not need to, you are so certain that God will bring it all out in perfect accordance with His will; John 14:1 ("let not your heart be troubled") has become the real state of your life. Until the resurrection life of Jesus Christ is manifested, we do want to ask questions; whenever we take a new step in God's providence we want to ask this and that. When the point of entire reliance on the resurrection of Jesus is reached, and we are brought into perfect contact with the purpose of God, we find all our questions have gone. Are we living that life now? If not, why shouldn't we?

What makes us say, "I wish God would tell me plainly"? Never look for an explanation from without or in your own mind; look for it in your disposition. The reason anything is a mystery and is coming in between yourself and God, is in the disposition, not in the intellect. When once the disposition is willingly submitted to the life of Jesus, the understanding becomes perfectly clear. "If anyone wants to do His will, he shall know concerning the doctrine."

THE TRANSFIGURED EXPERIENCE OF LIFE

"Suddenly, when they had looked around, they saw no one anymore, but only Jesus with themselves" (Mark 9:8).

There was no other moment, not even the resurrection of our Lord, so transcendent and amazing in the experience of Peter and James and John as the moment on the Mount of Transfiguration. Peter takes care to emphasize that it was when "we were with Him on the holy mountain" that he saw and heard and understood who Jesus was; we "were eyewitnesses of His majesty." In his epistle, James makes the practical application of this wonderful experience; and John, while he does not record the transfiguration, writes his gospel from this standpoint, the standpoint of the exceeding majesty of the Lord Jesus.

The Immortal Moments of Life

"Jesus . . . led them up on a high mountain apart by themselves; and He was transfigured before them" (Mark 9:2).

We all have what are called "brilliant moments." We are not always dull, not always contented with eating and drinking. There are times when we are unlike our usual selves, both in the way of depression and of brilliance, when one moment stands out from every other, and we suddenly see the way which we should go. And there is the counterpart in spiritual experience of those times in the natural life. There are tides of the spirit, immortal moments, moments of amazing clearness of vision; and it is by these moments and by what we see then, that we are to be judged. "While you have the light, believe in the light," said Jesus—do not believe what you see when you are not in the light. God is going to judge us by the times when we have been in living communion with Him, not by what we feel like today. God judges us entirely by what we have seen. We are not judged by the fact that we live up to the light of our conscience; we are judged by the Light, Jesus Christ. "I am the light of the world"; and if we do not know Jesus Christ, we are to blame. The only reason we do not know Him is because we have not bothered our heads about Him. Honestly, does it matter to us whether Jesus lived and died, or did anything at all? "But there are so many humbugs." There is no counterfeit without the reality. Is Jesus Christ a fraud? We are to be judged by Him. "This is the condemnation, that the light has come into the world, and men loved darkness rather than light." We are not judged by the light we have, but by the light we have refused to accept. God holds us responsible for what we will not look at. A man is never the same after he has seen Jesus. We are judged by our immortal moments, the moments in which we have seen the light of God.

The Isolation Moments of Life

". . . they were greatly afraid. And a cloud came and over-shadowed them" (Mark 9:6–7).

Something desolating, as well as something wonderful, happened to the disciples on the Mount of Transfiguration; they were transfixed with wonder at the sight of who Jesus was, then an isolating shadow came over them; they do not know the Jesus whom they are seeing now, and they are sore afraid, there is a chill over heart and life.

"For we do not wrestle against flesh and blood, but against principalities, against powers, against the rulers of the darkness of this age, against spiritual hosts of wickedness in the heavenly places." There is scenery surrounding the human soul of which we are unconscious, supernatural powers and agencies we know nothing about. Many a one has come to the place of the isolation moment, where it is cloudy and overshadowed. What are we going to do in these times of isolation? It would be an appalling thing to go through life unshielded by Jesus. We are inclined to be flippant, until God lifts the veil a little, then we get terrified. Let a little puff of wind blow over us, and instantly the "terror by night" isolates us in the alarm of the spirit. It is in these periods of isolation that our Lord keeps us. The atonement of Jesus means safeguarding in the unseen, safeguarding from dangers of which we know nothing.

Never be afraid because you do not understand yourself, and never be sour because no one else understands you. There is only one who understands us, and that is God (see Ps. 139). Our lives are lived in two compartments, the shallow and the profound, and both domains are to be God's. There is always the temptation to live only in the profound, and to despise others for not understanding our profundity. We are apt to forget that God is in the shallow as well as in the profound. We have to see that we live our shallow life in as godly a manner as we live the profound.

The Identified Meaning of Life

". . . they saw no one anymore, but only Jesus with themselves" (Mark 9:8).

It was not that they saw no one else, but they saw no one else without seeing Jesus. The identified meaning of life is that we see "every man perfect in Christ Jesus." We do not need a transfiguration experience to see meanness, because we are mean; we do not need a transfiguration experience to see sin, because we are sinners; but we do need a transfiguration experience to see Christ Jesus in the mean, in the sinner, in the all-but-lost, in the wrong and in the evil, so that it can be true of the experience of every saint—"they saw no one anymore, but only Jesus with themselves." That is what contact with Jesus means. It is easy to see the specks and the wrong in others, because we see in others that of which we are guilty ourselves. "Therefore you are inexcusable, O man, whoever you are who judge, for in whatever you judge another you condemn yourself; for you who judge practice the same things" (Rom. 2:1). The greatest cure for spiritual conceit is for God to give us a dose of the "plague of our own heart."

What a wonderful thing it will be for us if we enter into the transfigured experience of life! There is never any snare in the man or woman who has seen Jesus. Have you anyone "but only Jesus" in your cloud? If you have, then it will get darker. You must get to the place where there is "no one anymore, but only Jesus."

THE DAWN THAT
TRANSFIGURES TEARS

"Jesus said to her, 'Woman, why are you weeping?'" (John 20:15).

"And God will wipe away every tear from their eyes." Unless God wipes away our tears, they will always return. The day to which our Lord rose is a day in which tears are not done away with, but transfigured—a day that has no twilight, nor evening nor night. This does not mean that no more tears will be shed, but that they will never be shed again in the way they were before. We do not know what will take the place of tears, but a life in which there is no equivalent to tears would be intolerable to the imagination.

The Pressure of Pain in Termination

"He is not here" (Matt. 28:6).

The End of Three Years

". . . sitting opposite the tomb" (Matt. 27:61).

Those years had been a time of marvelous delight and joy, but they are finished now, and there is the pressure of pain in the termination of them. No greater sadness than that of the disciples can be imagined. They owed everything to Jesus, and now "He is not here," and life has nothing more to hold out for them. We have all had the equivalent of those three years, a time of great joy while it lasted, but it is finished now, and we too have sat "opposite the tomb."

The End of the Thrilling Yesterdays

"Then he went out and wept bitterly" (Matt. 26:75).

Peter was a loyal, strong, warm-hearted man, swayed by impulse; and now all the aspirations of his life have come to an end. We have all known the thrilling yesterday—when we first entered into the realization of love, or of friendship, or of the joy of life. If all that we have is the human, it will end in bitter tears—not sometimes, but every time. The only way in which bitter tears can be evaded is either by a man's shallowness, or by his coming into a totally new relation to the Lord Jesus Christ through His resurrection.

The End of Tender Yearnings

"What kind of conversation is this that you have with one another as you walk?" (Luke 24:17).

These words represent all we understand by tender yearnings. There are things in our lives that terminate; it is a universal human experience. Things come to an end and it produces unutterable sadness.

"He is not here." These are the saddest words on earth. Think what such words mean to mothers who have lost their sons in war, to wives who have lost their husbands. Yet in *this* connection they are extraordinarily joyful words—"He is not here; for He is risen." He is not here, in the ordinary sense of the word—not merely as one who can sympathize with sor-

row: He *is* here—but as the risen Lord! If we pour out sympathy upon one who is bereaved, all we do is to make that one
more submissive to his grief. The unique thing about Jesus is
that He comes to sorrowing men as a complete savior from all
sorrow.

The Power in the Proclamation of the Impossibilities

". . . for He is risen" (Matt. 28:6).

Jesus is not in the sitting by the tomb; He is not in the
bitter tears; He is not in the sad communings. The place where
we will find Jesus is just where common sense says it is impossible to find Him. It was no use for the disciples to imagine
they were going to have a recurrence of those three years; it
was impossible to recall the thrilling yesterdays; it was impossible for the two on the way to Emmaus to have a return of the
fellowship they yearned for; but there was something infinitely
better for them. "For He is risen, as He said." Impossibility had
wedded itself to what Jesus had said. The proclamation of the
impossible springs from the supernatural, not from common
sense. The supernatural figures largely all through the life of
our Lord. At His birth the angels proclaimed that He should be
called Jesus "for He will save His people from their sins." We
shall not think of our Lord as a savior if we look at Him in the
light of our own minds, because no natural man imagines he
needs to be saved. Do we make room in our faith for the
impossible along the line of the supernatural? or have we re-
duced our religion to such common sense platitudes that there
is no need for Jesus to have lived at all?

At His resurrection, the angel proclaimed, "He is not here;
for He is risen, as He said." The disciples' common sense would
tell them that what the angel said was an impossibility. Do we

believe the proclamation of the supernatural, or do we refuse to believe what we say is impossible? It is "impossible" for God to be born into human flesh; but Jesus was. It is "impossible" for a dead man to rise again; but Jesus rose. It is "impossible" for a man, even if he rose from the dead, to ascend into heaven; but Jesus did. When we reach the limit of what our common sense tells us can be done, then the word comes, "With God all things are possible." The limit of the possible means that God has a word of impossibility which He will perform in us if we have faith.

The Passing to the Path of Joy

"And go quickly . . . indeed He is going before you" (Matt. 28:7).

"He is not here"—not here in your limitations, not here in your way of looking at things; He is going before you all the time, and the rousing inspiration is, "go quickly and tell His disciples."

Think of the unspeakable thrill that must have come to the brokenhearted Mary Magdalene. She had had her thrilling yesterday, Jesus had cast out of her seven demons, and all her faith and hope was in Him; but He is dead. Now the angel proclaims that He is risen—"Do not be afraid . . . and go quickly and tell His disciples . . . ." All that stands for tears comes with limitation. When limitation touches us and the tears come, we are apt to say, "It is all finished now," and we are too dispirited to do anything. Then comes the inspiration—"Go quickly," get on your feet and go at once. It is not an inspiration according to common sense, but an arresting inspiration of astonishment. "Indeed He is going before you." We take the next step in limitation and are met with limitless divine power. We have to go as if God were not there, to take the first step without Him, and we find He is there all the time. We do not go alone, we go into the realization of the wonder of His presence. "Behold, I have told you." The supernatural character of the angel is at stake in the accepting of the inspiration. When we talk unguardedly to a child, we speak real truth because a child sees what no one else sees; when we talk to grown-up people we speak acquired common sense. We need to get back to the "angel" talk.

The Pledge of the Promise of Sight

". . . there you will see Him" (Matt. 28:7).

We shall not see Jesus if we sit still, or if we pray and long for Him, but if we go quickly, "there you will see Him." Go in your mind, rouse yourself up, indulge no more in reminiscent worship. That is a danger that persists until we realize that Jesus is risen not to the old life but to an inconceivably new life, and that our relationship to Him now is to be an altogether different one. "Do not cling to Me . . . but go to My brethren." We have to go on to the next thing, and there we shall see Him. We enthrone our reason and say, "seeing is believing." Have we the simple childlike faith to believe that if we do the next thing we shall see Him just there? To "wash one another's feet" is a commonplace thing to do, but it is there that we see Him. Do we believe in a perfect, present, absolute redemption—a redemption that is complete and finished? That redemption is the work of the risen Lord. His resurrection is the dawn that transfigures tears.

THE SACRAMENT OF SACRIFICE

"He who believes in Me . . . out of his heart will flow rivers of living water" (John 7:38).

Jesus Christ did not say, "He who believes in Me, in himself shall realize the blessing of the fullness of God," but, in effect, "out of him shall escape everything he has received." Our Lord always preaches anti-self-realization; He is not after developing a man at all, He is after making a man exactly like Himself, and the measure of the Son of God is self-expenditure. If we believe on Jesus Christ it is not what we gain but what He pours through us that counts. It is not that God makes us beautifully rounded grapes, but that He squeezes the sweetness out of us. We cannot measure our lives by spiritual success, but only by what God pours through us, and we cannot measure that at all. Who can measure the influence of a star or of a lily? Yet these are the things our Lord told us to consider. "He who believes in Me"—through him will He pour everything, leaving him nothing. A sacrament is the real presence in the actual elements; in this connection the actual elements are our lives.

The Waters of Satisfaction Scattered

"So the three mighty men broke through the camp of the
Philistines, drew water from the well of Bethlehem that was
by the gate, and took it and brought it to David. Nevertheless, he would not drink it, but poured it out to the LORD"
(2 Sam. 23:16).

I can never sanctify to God that with which I long to
satisfy myself. If I am going to satisfy myself with the blessings
of God, they will corrupt me; I have to sacrifice them, pour
them out, do with them what any commonsense man would
say is an absurd waste. Take it in the case of friendship, or of
blessing, or of spiritual experiences; as soon as I long to hold
any of these for myself I cannot sanctify them to the Lord.
David had the right idea when he poured out the water before
the Lord.

What has been like water from the well of Bethlehem to
you recently? Love, friendship, spiritual blessing? Then at the
peril of your soul, you take it to satisfy yourself. If you do, you
cannot pour out before the Lord. How am I to pour out spiritual gifts, or natural friendship, or love? How can I give them
to the Lord? In one way only—in the determination of my
mind, and that takes about two seconds. If I hold spiritual
blessings or friendship for myself they will corrupt me, no
matter how beautiful they are. I have to pour them out before
the Lord, give them to Him in my mind, though it looks as if I
am wasting them; even as when David poured the water out
on the sand, to be instantly sucked up.

There are certain acts of other people one could never
accept if one did not know God, because it is not within
human power to repay them, all we can do is to pour it out
before the Lord. If I take such a line as, "Oh, I am so winsome
they have to do this for me," I have turned it into poison, and it

cannot be consecrated to God. But as soon as I say, "This is too great and worthy a thing for me, it is not for a human being at all, I must pour it out before the Lord," then these things pour out in rivers of living water all around. Until we do pour these things out before the Lord they will always endanger those we love, because they turn to lust. We can be lustful in things that are not sordid and vile. Love has to get to its transfiguration point of being poured out before the Lord, otherwise it will get sordid. If you have gotten bitter and sour, you will probably find it is because God brought you a blessing and you clutched it for yourself; whereas if you had poured it out to the Lord, you would have been the sweetest person out of heaven. If we are craving spiritual sponges, always taking these things to ourselves, we shall become a plague; other people will not get their horizon enlarged through us because we have never learned to pour out anything unto the Lord.

The Way of Salvation

". . . because He poured out His soul unto death . . ." (Isa. 53:12).

This is the greatest love of God. No man ever laid down his life for his enemies unless he was indwelt by God. By the original design of God human nature is so built that men will always answer to the heroic. John 15:13 has reference to the love of man; that sacrifice is the exhibition of the sublime height to which human nature can rise with nothing of the love of God in it. Is Jesus Christ the Savior of the world to me, or am I so overtaken with delight and reverence at the sacrifice of men that I make the atonement of no account? Then the pleasure of the Lord is not possible in me, it only prospers in the hands of the man who makes his soul an offering. We too often make it salvation by preaching instead of preaching salvation. We have to work on the accomplished redemption of the world, and not for it; we are here to proclaim that God has delivered men from sin, not that a man by sacrifice can save his own soul. Our salvation comes to us so easily because it cost God so much.

The Waste of Sentiment

"And she broke the flask and poured it on His head" (Mark 14:3).

It was an act no one else saw any occasion for; they said it was a waste. It was not an extraordinary occasion, and yet Mary broke the box of ointment and spilled the whole thing. It was not a useful thing, but an act of extravagant devotion, and Jesus commended her and said wherever His gospel was preached, this also should be spoken of for a memorial of her.

God spilled the life of His Son that the world might be saved. Am I prepared to spill my life out for Him? Our Lord is carried beyond Himself with delight when He sees any of us doing what Mary did, extravagantly wasting our substance for Him; not set for this or that economy, but being abandoned to Him.

In the Bible there is always a oneness between the spiritual and the material. It takes the incarnation of the Holy Spirit in a man's body to make him what Jesus Christ wants him to be. Unless the blessings of God can deal with our bodies and make them the temples of the Holy Spirit, then the religion of Jesus Christ is in the clouds. If I cannot exhibit the sentiment of the Holy Spirit in the sordid actualities of life and in doing menial things from the highest motive, I am not learning to pour out unto the Lord.

"He who believes in Me . . . out of his heart will flow . . ."—not, he shall gain, but hundreds of others shall be continually refreshed. It is time now to break the life, to cease craving for satisfaction, and to spill the thing out. The Lord is asking for thousands of us to do it for Him.

SPIRITUAL DISCIPLESHIP

"For whoever desires to save his life will lose it, and whoever loses his life for My sake will find it" (Matt. 16:25).

"Spiritual" is used here in the sense of real, that is, that
which lies behind the actual and which we cannot get at by
our senses. In the beginning we call the actual things real; but
when we are born again we discern that reality and actuality
are not one and the same thing, and we understand the distinction Paul makes when he says, "the things which are seen are
temporary, but the things which are not seen are eternal." The
redemption of our Lord Jesus Christ is the great abiding reality;
to be spiritual disciples means that we have been brought into
experiential contact with redemptive reality by the power of
the grace of God.

The Source of Spiritual Discipleship

"For whoever desires to save his life [soul, KJV] will lose it."

Soul is my way of reasoning and looking at things, it is the
expression of my personal spirit in my body. Here our Lord is
saying, in effect, "If you are going to be My disciple, you must
lose your soul." Am I prepared to lose my soul? When I am
born from above and the redemption has been made experientially real in me by the Spirit of God, then I have to begin to

139

reason about things as Jesus did; I have to form the mind of Christ, and it will mean an about-face in every way. If I say I have always looked at things in this way and I always shall, then I will never become a spiritual disciple.

We are apt to confuse the strong-minded man with the obstinate man. An obstinate man refuses to be reasoned with; his argument is, "I have said it and I will stick to it." Spiritually the strong-minded man is one who has learned to construct his reasoning on the basis of the redemption; he faces every issue of life in the light of the Lord Jesus.

There is a difference between being saved and being a disciple. Some of us are saved, "yet so as through fire." We are grateful to God for saving us from sin, but we are of no use to Him in so far as our actual life is concerned. We are not spiritual disciples. Our Lord's last command was not, "Go and save men," but, "Go, . . . and make disciples." We cannot make disciples of others unless we are disciples ourselves. When a man comes to Jesus it is not sin that is in the way, but self-realization, pride, his claim to himself. "I must realize myself, I must be educated and trained, I must do those things that will help me to develop myself." Self-realization is anti-Christian. All this is vigorous paganism, it is not Christianity. Jesus Christ's attitude is always that of *anti*-self-realization. His purpose is not the development of man at all; His purpose is to make man exactly like Himself, and the characteristic of the Son of God is not self-realization but self-expenditure. Spiritual selfishness must go—am I prepared for it to go? "If any one desires to come after Me, let him deny himself," that is, "let him give up his right to himself to Me."

"Present your bodies a living sacrifice," says Paul. He does not say "present your all." "All" is an elusive word, because no one knows what his "all" is. Paul says, "Present your bodies . . . ." Do not ask God to take your body, but give your body to God. "I beseech you"—I passionately entreat you—says Paul, "present your bodies a living sacrifice." That is spiritual sacrifice. God does not ask us to give up things for the sake of giving them up; He asks us to sacrifice them, to give back to Him the best He has given us in order that it may belong to Him and us for ever. Sacrifice is the source of spiritual discipleship.

The Supremacy of Spiritual Discipleship

". . . and whoever loses his life for My sake will find it."

Many people lose their lives, but not for Christ's sake. "For My sake,"—that is the supreme surrender. God does not transform a man's life by magic, but through the surrender of the man to Himself. The thirteenth chapter of 1 Corinthians is the description of the way love works out in actual life. To most of us "love" is a curiously useless word. The love Paul refers to is the sovereign preference of my person for another person, and that other person is Jesus Christ. That sovereign preference works out in the deliberate identification of myself with God's interests in other people, and God is interested in some strange people; He is interested in the man whom I am inclined to despise.

As a spiritual disciple I have to lose my individuality forever. Individuality is self-assertive and independent, it is all elbows. It is natural for a child to be strongly marked by individuality, but it is a despicable thing for a man or woman to be hide-bound by individual peculiarities. It means that the personality has never been transfigured, never been filled with the Holy Spirit, never come to the source of spiritual reality. Our Lord can only be defined in terms of personality, never in terms of individuality. "I and My Father are one," and our Lord's conception of human personality is that it can be

141

merged and made one with God without losing its identity. If we are going to be disciples we have to break the bands of individuality which cabin and confine, and launch out in abandon to Jesus Christ.

We cannot get at reality by thinking or by emotion, but only by conscience, and the Spirit of God working through conscience brings a man straight to the redemptive reality of our Lord, then there follows a life of spiritual discipleship, pouring out for others for His sake. The saint must become like his master, utterly unobtrusive. For "we do not preach ourselves, but Christ Jesus the Lord, and ourselves your servants for Jesus' sake." If you are serving men for their sakes you will soon have the heart knocked out of you; but if you are personally and passionately devoted to the Lord Jesus Christ, then you can spend yourselves to the last ebb because your motive is love to the Lord.

We never want Jesus Christ in the actual turmoil of life unless we have found Him in the real, but when we have found Him there He brings into actual life a transfiguring touch. He makes the real and the actual one. Jesus Christ is the at-one-ment, and I can only get the atonement made real in me by being born from above into the realm Jesus Christ came to lift me into. God grant we may be among those who are prepared to be spiritual disciples. As disciples we must give up spiritual selfishness; we must make the spiritual sacrifice of presenting our bodies to God, and we must live the superlative life of being identified with God's interests in other people.

SACRAMENTAL DISCIPLESHIP

"Christ did not send me to baptize but to preach the gospel. And to preach it with no fine rhetoric, lest the Cross of Christ should lose its power!" (1 Cor. 1:17–18, Moffatt).

The word "sacrament" is used in connection with the Lord's Supper and means the real presence of God coming through the actual elements. The real presence of God is brought to us also in the actual things of life by means of the sacramental element in redemption. It is a trick of our minds to think that God and actual things are one and the same; God comes to us in actual things, but actual things are not God. "In everything give thanks," says Paul, not, "Give thanks *for* everything," but give thanks that in everything that transpires there abides the real presence of God. God is more real than the actual things—"therefore we will not fear, though the earth be removed." We think that our actual life is profound until something happens—a war or a bereavement, and we are flung clean abroad, then through the agony of the mystery of life we cry out to God and there comes the voice of Jesus— "Come to Me."

The Sacrament of the Historic Cross

"Christ did not send me to baptize"—to put religious rites in the front—"but to preach the gospel." The gospel is not so much good news to man as good news about God. "And to preach it with no fine rhetoric." It is one thing to thrill an audience with fine rhetoric, or by a magnetic personality, but the New Testament order of preaching is that of John the Baptist—"He must increase, but I must decrease." The one thing for Paul was Christ and Him crucified, not Christ risen and exalted, but Christ "crucified." Paul had only one passion, and that was the exposition and the emphasis and the re-emphasis of the cross. The New Testament emphasizes the death of Christ because the cross is the center that reveals the very heart of God. The death Jesus died was not the death of a martyr, it was the revelation in actual history of the very nature of God. "But we preach Christ crucified, to Jews a stumbling block," a distress and a humiliation "and to the Greeks" (those who seek wisdom), "foolishness, but to those who are called, both Jews and Greeks, Christ the power of God and the wisdom of God."

It seems so remote from actual things to say that the preaching of the cross conveys the presence of God, but God has chosen to save in this way. "It pleased God through the foolishness of the message preached to save those who believe," because behind the preaching of the gospel is the creative redemption of God at work in the souls of men. That is the miracle of God. If you can tell how a corn of wheat when put into the ground will bring forth what it never was before, you can also tell how the Word of God put into a man's soul will bring forth what was not there before—a new life. The same God is the author of both. How are men born of the Spirit? By the proclaiming of the historic cross of Christ. "The wind blows where it wishes . . . . So is everyone who is born of the Spirit." The simple proclaiming of the gospel of God creates the need for the gospel. Nothing can satisfy the need but that which creates the need. The inner reality of redemption is that it creates all the time. "And I, if I am lifted up from the earth, will draw all peoples to Myself." Once let Jesus be lifted up and the Spirit of God creates the need for Him.

Unless we are born from above, the cross of Christ means nothing to us; it does not matter whether Jesus lived or died; the New Testament is an exquisitely beautiful record of a life, but it *conveys* nothing. The words of Isaiah 53:2 are humiliatingly true of us all. When we see the Highest, He is to us as a root out of a dry ground, thoroughly disadvantaged. When the religious people of His day saw the Highest incarnate before them, they hated Him and crucified Him. It is only when a man gets to his wits' end and is stabbed wide awake that he realizes for the first time the meaning of the cross—"I thought that He was stricken, smitten by God and afflicted; now I see that He was wounded for my transgression."

"The Lamb slain from the foundation of the world." In the cross God is revealed not as one reigning in calm disdain above all the squalors of earth, but as one who suffers more keenly than the keenest sufferer—"a Man of sorrows and acquainted with grief." This rules out once and for all the idea that Jesus was a martyr. Jesus did not die the death of a martyr; He died the death not of a good man, but the death due to a bad man, with the vicarious pain of Almighty God at His heart. That pain is unfathomable to us, but we get an insight into it in the cry upon the cross, "My God, My God, why have You forsaken Me?" The death of Jesus goes away down underneath the deepest, vilest sin that human nature ever committed. Every pious mood must be stripped off when we stand before the cross. The cross in actual history is the point where the real presence of God enters human history; and the point where the real presence of God enters human life is the moment of abso-lute surrender, not of religious sentiment. The first step to sacramental discipleship is the crowning of Jesus as Lord.

The Sacrament of the Scriptures

"You search the Scriptures, for in them you think you have eternal life; and these are they which testify of Me" (John 5:39).

The context of the Bible is the Lord Jesus Christ. The Scriptures do not give us life unless Jesus speaks them to us. Jesus Christ makes His words "spirit and life" to us if we will obey them. If we are not born again the Word of God is nothing to us. When men tear this book of God to pieces it reveals how blind they are. To the saint this book of God is a sacrament, it conveys the real presence of God. God by His providence puts needs in our actual life which drive us to search the Scriptures, and as we search them, the sacrament of God's presence comes to us through the words of His book.

The Sacrament of the Saint

"Do you love Me? . . . Feed My sheep" (John 21:15–17).

A saint must measure his life by self-expenditure, that is, by what God pours through him. Just as the real presence of God comes through the preaching of the crucified Christ, and through the words of the Bible, so it comes through His chil-dren. "Do you love Me? . . . Feed My sheep"—and Jesus gave Peter nothing to feed them with. The disciple has himself to be the very bread of God by the power of the redemption at work in him. Just as our Lord was made broken bread and poured out wine for our salvation, so He makes us broken bread in His hands. Thank God for all those who are sacramental saints; they have been through the furnace with God, and the presence of God comes through their actual lives.

The secret of sacramental discipleship is to be so abandoned to the disposition of God in us that He can use us as broken bread and poured out wine for His purpose in the world, even as He broke the life of His own Son to redeem us.

THE LIMIT OF DEDICATION

"She has done what she could" (Mark 14:8).

Mary Magdalene, the woman who was a sinner, and Mary of Bethany, the one who made this spontaneous dedication to Jesus, represent the three types of womanhood for whom Jesus Christ is sufficient—the tortured, the worst, and the best. Mary of Bethany stands as the noblest type of womanhood in our Lord's day. Her counterpart is the rich young ruler, but he failed in relation to Jesus Christ exactly where Mary did not fail.

The Unconscious Spontaneity of Love

". . . as He sat at the table, a woman came having an alabaster flask of very costly oil of spikenard. And she broke the flask and poured it on His head" (Mark 14:3).

If human love is always discreet and calculating, never carried beyond itself, it is not of the true nature of love. The characteristic of love is that it is spontaneous, it bursts up in extraordinary ways; it is never premeditated. The reason Jesus called Mary's act "a good work" was because it was wrought out of spontaneous love to Himself. It was neither useful nor her duty; it was an extravagant act for which no one else saw any occasion. "But Jesus said, 'Let her alone. Why do you trouble her? She has done a good work for Me.'" The disciples were indignant—"Why was this fragrant oil wasted?"—"If she had only sold the ointment and given us the money, we would have used it for the poor." Money is one of the touch- stones in our Lord's teaching. Today we are taken up with our ideas of economy and thrift, and never see that those ideas are not God's ideas. The very nature of God is extravagance. How many sunrises and sunsets does God make?

Gloriously wasteful, O my Lord, art Thou!
Sunset faints after sunset into the night . . . .

How many flowers and birds, how many inexpressable beauties all over the world, lavish desert blossoms, that only His eye sees? Mary's act was one of spontaneous extravagance because it sprang out of the heart of a child. When our Lord said, "Unless you . . . become as little children . . ." He was not setting up a little child as a standard, but as the exact expression of an implicit relationship to Himself.

The Unconscious Sympathy of Life

"For you have the poor with you always, and whenever you wish you may do them good; but Me you do not have al- ways. She has done what she could. She has come be- forehand to anoint My body for burial" (Mark 14:7–8).

Jesus is pointing out that the great note of our lives as His disciples is not sympathy with the poor, not an understanding of the needs of men, but an understanding of His point of view. "Watch with Me"; "Give Me a drink"; "Continue with Me." No one can understand Jesus Christ's point of view unless he has His Spirit. The need is never the call; the need is the opportunity. The call is defined in John 17:18—"As You sent Me into the world, I also have sent them into the world." The first obedience of our Lord was not to the needs of men but to the will of His Father; and our first obedience is to Jesus Christ, not to the poor and the despised and afflicted. My sympathy with them is the proof that I have a loving sympathy greater than them all, namely, sympathy with my Lord. Mary of Bethany revealed in her act of extravagant devotion that the unconscious sympathy of her life was with Jesus Christ. "She has done what she could"—to the absolute limit of what a woman can do. It was impossible to do more.

"She has come beforehand to anoint My body for burial." Mary did not know that she was anointing the body of Jesus for His burial. Her heart was bursting with love to Jesus, and she took this opportunity of giving it expression. Love is the sovereign preference of my person for another person, and if I am a disciple of Jesus, that sovereign preference is for Him. "O forgotten and neglected Jesus, my eyes have looked on You." That means I am spoiled for everything saving as I can be used to glorify Him.

The Unconscious Service of Loyalty

Mark 14:9

The only thing Jesus ever commended was this act of Mary's, and He said, "Wherever this gospel is preached throughout the whole world, what this woman did will also be spoken of as a memorial to her," because in the anointing our Lord saw an exact illustration of what He Himself was about to do. He put Mary's act alongside His own cross. God shattered the life of His own Son to save the world; are we prepared to pour out our lives for Him? Our Lord is carried beyond Himself with joy when He sees any of us doing what Mary of Bethany did. The one thing He looks for in a disciple is abandon. Abandon to God is of more value than personal holiness. Personal holiness focuses our eyes on our own whiteness; when we are abandoned to God, He works through us all the time. When David's three mighty men brought him the water from the well of Bethlehem, we read that "he would not drink it, but poured it out to the LORD." David saw in their devotion something worthy only to be poured out before God.

Have I ever produced in the heart of the Lord Jesus what Mary of Bethany produced? "She has done what she could"— to the absolute limit. I have not done what I could until I have done the same.

THE SPIRITUAL "D.S.O."

"If anyone serves Me, let him follow Me; and where I am, there My servant will be also. If anyone serves Me, him My Father will honor" (John 12:26).

The Service of Passionate Devotion

"If anyone serves Me, let him follow Me."

Our idea of service is often the outcome of devotion to a principle, but Jesus is here dealing with the service that is devotion to Him. With us, Christian service is something we do; with Jesus Christ it is not what we *do for* Him, but what we *are to* Him that He calls service. Our Lord always puts the matter of discipleship on the basis of devotion not to a belief or a creed, but to Himself. There is no argument about it, and no compulsion, simply, if you would be His disciple, you must be devoted to Him.

The Source of Devotion

"'What shall we do, that we may work the works of God?' . . . 'This is the work of God, that you believe in Him . . .'" (John 6:28–29).

Where is the devotion to spring from? "Believe also in Me." Do I believe Jesus, not believe about Him, but believe

Him? Peter, when he confessed that our Lord was the Son of God, was talking out of the spontaneous originality of his own heart. With a tremendous amazement he said, "You are the Christ, the Son of the living God," and instantly Jesus says, "Blessed are you," you did not guess it, it was an intuition from My Father, "and on this rock [the rock of the revelation in personal life of who I am] I will build My church."

Have I realized who Jesus is to me? We substitute credal belief for personal belief. The intuitive heart of a man is suddenly touched by the Spirit of God and he says, "Now I see who Jesus is," and that is the source of devotion.

The Secret of Disaster

"He who is a hireling . . . flees . . ." (John 10:12).

Am I out for my own? Am I utilizing membership of the Christian church to further my own ends? If a preacher uses his position to further his own ends, he is heading for disaster. There are many devoted to causes, but few devoted to Jesus Christ. If I am devoted to a particular cause only, when that cause fails I fail too. The secret of a disciple's life is devotion to Jesus Christ, and the very nature of the life is that it is unobtrusive; it falls into the ground and dies: but presently it springs up and alters the whole landscape (see John 12:24). The illustrations Jesus uses are always drawn from his Father's work—"Consider the lilies of the field—look at the birds of the air"—not things with tangible external results, but lilies and birds, things with nothing pretentious about them.

The Spring of Direction

"Do you love Me? . . . Feed My sheep" (John 21:15–17).

If you love Me, says Jesus, "Feed My sheep." In other words, "Don't make converts to your way of thinking, but look after My sheep, see that they are nourished in the knowledge of Me." Our Lord's first obedience was to the will of His Father, and He said, "As the Father has sent Me, I also send you." It sounds the right thing to say that Jesus Christ came here to help mankind; but His great desire was to do the will of His Father, and our Lord was misunderstood because He would not put the needs of men first. He said the first commandment is, "You shall love the LORD your God with all your heart, with all your soul, and with all your mind, and with all your strength."

Jesus Christ is a source of deep offense to the educated trained mind of today that does not want Him in any other way than as a comrade. Many do not want to be devoted to Him, but only to the cause He started. If I am only devoted to the cause of humanity, I will be soon exhausted and come to the point where my love will falter, but if I love Jesus Christ I will serve humanity, though men and women treat me like a doormat.

The Society of Personal Dedication

". . . and where I am, there My servant will be also."

Anywhere the man who is devoted to Jesus Christ goes, Jesus Christ is there with him.

Felicity of Faithfulness

"Well done, good and faithful servant . . . enter into the joy of your lord" (Matt. 25:23).

The joy of a thing lies in fulfilling the purpose of its creation. Jesus Christ's joy is that He fulfilled the design of His Father's will, and my joy is that I fulfill God's design in calling me, that is, to make me a follower of Him.

Fullness of Following

> "If anyone loves Me, he will keep My word; and My Father will love him, and We will come to him and make Our home with him" (John 14:23).

Here is the description of the society of a man devoted to Jesus Christ in this actual life, whether in a camp or an office or the desert. Imagine the sublime society of a man—he has God the Father, God the Son, and God the Holy Spirit with him wherever he goes.

Fruitfulness of Friendship

> "I have called you friends" (John 15:15).

The fruitfulness of friendship is described in verse 13: "Greater love has no one than this, than to lay down one's life for his friends." If I am a friend of Jesus Christ, I lay down my life for Him. That does not mean that I go through the big crisis of death; it means that I lay down my life deliberately as I would lay out a pound note. I have this to lay out and expend: I have a day before me, and I am going to lay it out for Jesus Christ; I have my duty to perform, but I am going to lay it out in devotion to Jesus Christ all through. It is difficult, and thank God it is difficult. Salvation is easy because it cost God so much, but the manifestation of it in my life is difficult. God does expect a man to be a man. God saves a man and endues him with His Holy Spirit, and says in effect, "Now it is up to you to prove it, work it out; be loyal to Me while the nature of things round about you would make you disloyal. I have called you friends, now stand loyal to your Friend." His honor is at stake in our bodily life.

The Seal of Perfect Discipline

". . . if anyone serves Me, him My Father will honor."

If it were necessary for every man to lay down his life in a heroic way, as men have done in Gallipoli and in Flanders, what about the men and women who never get a chance of doing anything heroic? Everybody is not noble or generous or great; a great number of men are despicable beings. Is God going to put them on the scrap heap? "If you confess Me," Jesus says, as it were, "God Almighty will give you the D.S.O.—not if you are a good man, or have done wonderful things, but if you have served Me."

The Drill in Purity

"These are the ones who follow the Lamb wherever He goes" (Rev. 14:4).

Actually pure in their natural walk, they followed the Lamb in their actual lives, and were consciously redeemed by the blood of Christ. There is a difference between innocence and purity. Innocence is the characteristic of a child, purity is the characteristic of a man or woman who knows what the tendencies and temptations to go wrong are, and who has overcome them. Virtue is not in the man who has not been tempted, neither is purity. When a man is tempted and remains steadfastly unspotted, then he is virtuous.

Jesus Christ says in effect, "If you will serve Me, you will keep your chastity," that means there has to be a fight; you realize that all the power of God is behind you as you make the fight. You may be pure and unsullied for months, when all of a sudden there will be the insinuation of an idea; grip it on the threshold of your mind in a vice instantly, and do not allow it any more. If I am to serve Jesus Christ, I have to remember that my body is the temple of the Holy Spirit. Talk about it being a "soft" thing to be a follower of Jesus Christ! It is about the sternest and most heroic thing a man ever "struck" in his life to keep himself absolutely undefiled, one who by chastity maintains his integrity. It is a discipline, and thank God for the discipline.

The Duty of Patience

> "Because you have kept My command to persevere [the word of My patience, KJV] I also will keep you from the hour of trial which shall come upon the whole world, to test those who dwell on the earth" (Rev. 3:10).

Jesus says we are to keep the word of His patience. There are so many things in this life that it seems much better to be impatient about. The best illustration is that of an archer: he pulls the string further and further away from his bow with the arrow fixed, then, when it is adjusted, with his eye on the mark he lets fly. The Christian's life is like that. God is the archer; He takes the saint like a bow which He stretches, and we get to a certain point and say, "I can't stand any more, I can't stand this test of patience any longer," but God goes on stretching. He is not aiming at our mark, but at His own, and the patience of the saints is that we hold on until He lets the arrow fly straight to His goal.

PAIN IN THE DAWN OF ETERNAL HOPE

"For our light affliction, which is but for a moment, is working for us a far more exceeding and eternal weight of glory"
(2 Cor. 4:17).

The basis of human life is tragedy. It is difficult to realize
this until one gets through the experiences that are on the
surface of life, and we discover we are built with a bigger
capacity for pain than for joy, that the undertone of all our life
is sorrow, and the great expression and revelation of God in
the world is the revelation of the cross, not of joy. It is one of
the things which makes the Bible seem so utterly unreal so
long as we are healthy and full of life and spirits. Tragedy is
something in which all the forces make for disaster. Paul in
writing about human life always wrote from the Bible standpoint, which is, that the basis of things is not reasonable but
tragic. Sin has made a gap between God and the human race,
and consequently when we try to explain our lives on the line
of logic or reason, we find things don't work out that way.
Then when we go through disasters such as are being produced by this war, we are more prepared to look at the Bible
and its point of view. Jesus Christ stands outside the majority
of our lives in the usual run because He deals with the funda-
mentals; we do not, we deal with the external actuals, and it is

only when the external actuals are plowed into by sorrow or bereavement that we begin to find there is only one reality— our Lord Jesus Christ, and only one book that brings light.

Our Life in Tragedy

"Even though our outward man is *perishing*"—not *may perish*, but our outward man is built that way. That in itself is a tragedy; a beautiful physical life, a beautiful child's life, is all built at present on decay. It makes us rebel and produces almost spite against the Creator, but the Bible reveals that the reason for it all is the hiatus between God and man caused by sin.

Pain of Sensibility

"I will greatly multiply your sorrow" (Gen. 3:16).

We are introduced into this order of things by pain to someone else, not necessarily pain to ourselves but pain to our mothers. The basis of the bearing into this life of sensibility is pain. This is a fundamental revelation in God's book.

Pain of Salvation

"For Christ also suffered once for sins, the just for the unjust, that He might bring us to God, being put to death in the flesh but made alive by the Spirit" (1 Pet. 3:18).

The phrase, "born from above" as our Lord used it does not mean being saved from hell or from sin, but that I am born into the realm in which He lives. We are born again by pain, not necessarily pain to ourselves any more than our natural birth means pain to us. We are born into the realm where our Lord lives by pain to God, and the pain of God is exhibited on Calvary.

> "I have been crucified with Christ; it is no longer I who live,
> but Christ lives in me; and the life which I now live in the
> flesh I live by faith in the Son of God, who loved me and
> gave Himself for me" (Gal. 2:20).

We are dealing with fundamental pain, the basis of which
is tragedy—all the forces making for disaster. "I have been
crucified with Christ"—crucifixion is a painful thing. It
means, not in the theological sense, but in the spiritual sense,
being made one with Jesus Christ, and that costs *me* pain. I
have deliberately to be willing to give up my right to myself;
that has now been put to death by mine own determination,
and "the life which I now live in the flesh I live by faith in the
Son of God." Literally, the faith that was in Jesus Christ is
now in me.

These are the three big fundamental things in our human
life, and the basis of each is pain. They are not things to preach
about, but rather matters for our consideration. In the light of
this terrible tragedy of war where pain is sweeping the whole
universe until there is scarcely a home that has not been
touched by it, there is again a chance to witness the incoming
of the quiet power of our Lord Jesus Christ. I do not believe we
shall see the incoming power of denominationalism or
"Churchianity" or creed; but I do believe that the Spirit of God
is pushing His way into people's lives on the only line of
emancipation there is, namely, through the cross, and we are
realizing that the revelation given to us of God is of a God who
suffers. We see more into the real tragedy of life when we have
been hit hard by bereavement or unrequited love, or by some
great elemental pain that has shocked the externals. The human mind instantly says, "Why should these things be?" They
are unreasonable. Emphatically so, we may rage as we choose,

but we come to the conclusion that the Bible is right—the basis of things is tragic, not mathematical. As soon as we recognize that life is based on tragedy, we won't be too staggered when tragedy emerges, but will learn how to turn to God.

Our Light in Tragedy

"For our light affliction which is but for a moment, is working for us a far more exceeding and eternal weight of glory."

Where are we to get our light in all this appalling tragedy? It is obvious nonsense to say that suffering makes saints; it makes some people devils. Hebrews 12:11 is referring to the suffering that comes to a person who is being exercised by the Spirit of God. We all know people who have been made much meaner and more irritable and more intolerable to live with by suffering: it is not right to say that all suffering perfects. It only perfects one type of person—the one who accepts the call of God in Christ Jesus.

Undiscouraged by Decay

"Therefore we do not lose heart. Even though our outward man is perishing, yet the inward man is being renewed day by day" (2 Cor. 14:16).

There is nothing, naturally speaking, that makes us lose heart quicker than decay—the decay of bodily beauty, of natural life, of friendship, of associations, all these things make a man lose heart; but Paul says when we are trusting in Jesus Christ these things do not find us discouraged, light comes through them. "For we do not preach ourselves, but Christ Jesus the Lord, and ourselves your servants for Jesus' sake." That is the rock on which Paul stands, and that is where he gets his light. It does not matter what happens; there may be disasters or calamities or wars or bereavements and heart-breaks, but the marvelous thing in the man who is rightly related to Jesus Christ is that he is not discouraged. That is supernatural, no human being can stand these shocks and not be discouraged unless he is upheld by the supernatural grace of God. The counterfeit of true spirituality is that produced by creeds. When one has been bereaved the most trying person is the one with a creed who can come with didactic counsel with regard to suffering; but turn to a book like the book of Job where nothing is taught at all, but wonderful expression is given to the real suffering of life, and the mere reading of it brings consolation to a breaking heart. The standards of personal relationship to Jesus Christ leave a man undiscouraged by decay. The books and the men who help us most are not those who teach us, but those who can express for us what we feel inarticulate about.

Undeceived by Disillusionment

There are times in sorrow when we are disillusioned, our eyes are opened, and we see people in their true relationships, and often we get completely disheartened and feel we won't trust anyone any more. But when we are trusting to our Lord Jesus Christ, this kind of light affliction leaves us with a true discernment, we are not deceived, we see men and women in their right relationship, and light comes all through. Whatever happens, our relationship to Jesus Christ works through it. We have to learn to take up pain and weave it into the fabric of our lives.

Undistracted by Discernment

"While we do not look at the things which are seen, but at the things which are not seen. For the things which are seen

are temporary, but the things which are not seen are eternal"
(2 Cor. 4:18).

The things we see are actual, but not eternal, and the curious thing about actual things is that we cannot see the real, eternal things without them. The fanatic won't have actual things at all; he pretends he can see God and God's purposes apart from actual present circumstances. That is not so, we only see by means of the actual, and when we are going through the experience of the actual, we come to tragedy and sorrow and difficulty, but if we are trusting in God, we are undistracted by it.

Our Love in Tragedy

"While we . . . look . . . at the things which are not seen."

That is the description of love.

The Blindness of Insight

Love is not blind. Love has insight, it sees the things that are not seen. We are told that when we are in love with a person we do not see his defects; the truth is that we see what others do not see, we see him in the ideal, in the real relationship. The actual things in life are sordid and decaying and wrong and twisted, but we do not look at them, we look at the eternal things beyond, and the consequence is that in the actual tribulations and circumstances of the moment, pain works for us an eternal hope. We have all had the experience that it is only in the days of affliction that our true interests are furthered.

The Blundering of Intellect

The intellect only looks for things that are seen and actual, draws its inferences from these and becomes pessimistic and loses heart.

is that we know that "the things which are not seen are eternal." Love, joy, peace, these things are not seen, yet they are eternal, and God's nature is made up of these things. "The Lamb opened . . . the seals"—the eternal and abiding gentleness of God undoes everything.

"Our light affliction . . . ." To escape affliction is a cowardly thing to do; to sink under it is natural; to get at God through it is a spiritual thing. Most of us have tried the first, a good many of us have known the second, and the Spirit of God in us knows the third, getting through into the weight of glory. That means we become people of substance spiritually; we can be relied on when others are in pain or sorrow, and after this war is done there will be a call for every one of us to be of use for God in that direction, not to be didactic and set on our own views, but simply to be ourselves rightly related to our Lord Jesus Christ so that through us the presence of God may come to others. Rational common sense talk does not deal with eternal things, and is an insult when we are dealing with the things that are not seen. We have to learn to live in the reality of the eternal things.

Y.M.C.A. Hut, 5 November 1916

THE HONOR OF A SAINT

Galatians 2:20

Redemption is the basis of things, it is God's "bit"; we have to live our actual life on that basis. We are apt to get a conception of the redemption that enables us to "hang in" to Jesus mentally and do nothing else. This seems the natural outcome of the way redemption has too often been presented. God expects us to maintain in our individual lives the honor of a saint. It is up to us to live the life of a saint in order to show our gratitude to God for His amazing salvation, a salvation which cost us nothing but which cost God everything.

In this passage Paul describes how this point of honor was reached in his life—"I have been crucified with Christ . . . and the life which I now live in the flesh . . . ." The word "now" is very annoying, if only Paul had said "hereafter"—"this is the kind of life I am going to live after I am dead and in heaven; down here I am compassed about with infirmities and am a miserable sinner." But he did not, he said "*now*," "the life which I now live in the flesh"—that is, the life men could see. ". . . I live by faith in the Son of God."

165

The Moral Death of Self-Will

"I have been crucified with Christ . . . ."

Paul is referring to a deliberate act on his own part, he has given over to death his self-will. Will is "me" active, not one bit of me but the whole of me. Self-will is best described as the whole of myself active around my own point of view, and Paul is speaking of moral death to that—he says, in effect, "I have deliberately identified myself with the death of Jesus, and I no longer work around my own point of view." The reference to the death of Christ is not merely to our Lord's sacrificial death with which we have nothing to do—the death of Jesus is the death of God on the plane of human history for one purpose, the justification of the holiness of God and the manifestation of the true nature of God—Paul is stating as a fact that he has morally identified himself with that death. For us it means that we deliberately and actually identify ourselves with the death of Jesus, and accept God's verdict on the things which He condemns in that death; in other words, we deliberately give up our right to ourselves to God. Whenever our Lord speaks about discipleship, it is this point He emphasizes—"If any man desires to come after Me, let Him deny himself"—that is, let him give up his right to himself. No one can bring us to this denial, even God Himself cannot, we must come there of our own accord, and the length of time it takes to do so depends entirely on whether we want to come or not. If we give way to the play of our emotions and do not intend deliberately to come to the point of identification, we will get off on to spiritual sentimentality and end nowhere.

Disentangling the Inner Life

"Then Simon Peter answered Him, 'Lord, to whom shall we go? You have the words of eternal life'" (John 6:68).

166

John 6 contains a description of the sifting out of the disciples from the crowd round about, until there were just the twelve left, and to them Jesus says, "Do you also want to go away?" Some who had been following Jesus had not gone too far to turn back, and "Many of His disciples went back and walked with Him no more." But Peter has gone too far to turn back and he says, "Lord, to whom shall we go?" There is a stage like that in our spiritual experience; we do not see the guide ahead of us, we do not feel the joy of the Lord, there is no exhilaration, yet we have gone too far to go back, we are up against it now. It might be illustrated in the spiritual life by Tennyson's phrase, "a white funeral." When we go through the moral death to self-will we find we have committed ourselves, there are many things that must go to the "white funeral." At the first we have the idea that everything apart from Christ is bad; but there is much in our former life that is fascinating, any amount of paganism that is clear and vigorous, virtues that are good morally. But we have to discover they are not stamped with the right image and superscription, and if we are going to live the life of a saint we must go to the moral death of those things, make a termination of them, turn these good natural things into the spiritual.

Disciplining the Intuitive Light

"While you have the light, believe in the light, that you may become sons of light" (John 12:36).

Intuition in the natural world means that we see or discern at sight, there is no reasoning in connection with it, we see at once. When the Spirit of God is in us He gives us intuitive discernment, we know exactly what He wants; then the point is, are we going through identification with our Lord in order that that intuitive light may become the discipline of our lives?

167

It is this practical aspect that has been ignored. We have not sufficiently emphasized the fact that we have to live as saints, and that in our lives the honor at stake is not our personal honor, but the honor of Jesus Christ.

When we are beginning to be spiritual by means of the reception of the Holy Spirit, we get moments of intuitive light. We are not always dull, there are moments when we are brilliant, and Jesus says, "While you have the light, believe in the light." We are apt to believe what we saw in the dark, and consequently we believe wrongly. We have to believe what we saw when we were in the light, "hang in" to it, discipline the whole of our lives up to it. If the Holy Spirit is working in our hearts, all this becomes implicitly clear to us. The Holy Spirit is honest, and we know intuitively whether we have or have not been identified with the death of Jesus, whether we have or have not given over our self-will to the holy will of God.

Discovering the Inspired Loyalty

"Do you love Me? . . . Feed My sheep . . ." (John 21:15–18).

When we do decide to go to the death of self-will, we discover that the inspired loyalty of our lives is devotion to Jesus. "Do you love Me?" Then, "feed my sheep." Jesus did not say, "Go out and spread propaganda," but, "feed My sheep." They are not our sheep, but His. We are apt to take loyalty to convictions to be the same as loyalty to Christ. Convictions mean a great deal in our mental makeup, but there are stages when conscience and Christ are antagonistic. Paul said, "Indeed, I myself thought I must do many things contrary to the name of Jesus of Nazareth" (Acts 26:9). Inspired loyalty is not loyalty to my attitude to the truth, but loyalty to the truth—

Jesus Christ. Conscience simply means that power in me that affiliates itself with the highest I know; if I do not know Jesus, then my conscience will not be loyal to God as revealed in Him. It is possible for conscience and Christ to go together, but it is not necessarily so. We see saints hard and metallic because they have become loyal to a phase of truth, instead of remembering that Jesus does not send His disciples out to advocate certain phases of truth, but to feed His sheep and tend His lambs. The inspired loyalty is to Jesus Himself.

Verse 18 is the symbol of the moral death of self-will. "When you were younger, you girded yourself and walked where you wished; but when you are old . . . another will gird you and carry you where you do not wish." When we are young in the spiritual life we do practically exactly what we want to do, then there comes a time when we have to face this question of moral death to self-will. Am I determined to go through the discipline of identification with my Lord's point of view and no longer make my own point of view the center of my life? If I am going to maintain the honor of a saint, I have deliberately to go to the death of my self-will.

The Moral Discipline of Spiritual Will

". . . it is no longer I who live, but Christ lives in me."

The Blood of Christ

"But if we walk in the light as He is in the light, we have fellowship with one another, and the blood of Jesus Christ His Son cleanses us from all sin" (1 John 1:7).

When we speak of the blood of Jesus Christ cleansing us from all sin, we do not mean the physical blood shed on Calvary, but the whole life of the Son of God which was poured out to redeem the world. All the perfections of the essential nature of God were in that blood, and all the holiest attain-ments of mankind as well. It was the life of the perfection of deity that was poured out on Calvary, ". . . the church of God which He purchased with His own blood" (Acts 20:28). We are apt to look upon the blood of Jesus Christ as a magic-working power instead of its being the very life of the Son of God poured forth for men. The whole meaning of our being identified with the death of Jesus is that His blood may flow through our mortal bodies. Identification with the death of Jesus Christ means identification with Him to the death of everything that never was in Him, and it is the blood of Christ, in the sense of the whole personal life of the Son of God, that comes into us and "cleanses us from all sin."

The Blood of Personality

"That I may know Him and the power of His resurrection, and the fellowship of His sufferings, being conformed to His death" (Phil. 3:10).

Paul's whole personality was passionately devoted to Jesus—"that I may know Him." As soon as that note domi-nates a personality everything is simplified. It is impossible for the natural man once born, to have a single motive. We know when the love of God has been shed abroad in our hearts because of this miracle of a single motive. The moral discipline of spiritual will is that I rerelate myself all through according to this motive. It is no longer my claim to my right to myself that rules my personal life—I am not dead, but the old disposi-tion of my right to myself has gone, it is Jesus Christ's right to me that rules me now, "and the life which I now live in the flesh" I live from that center. The attitude of a saint is that he is related to God through Jesus Christ, consequently the spring of his life is other than the world sees.

"If you abide in Me, and My words abide in you, you will ask what you desire, and it shall be done for you" (John 15:7).

". . . and whatever you ask in My name, that I will do" (John 14:13).

". . . Ask what you desire"—That is, not what you like, but ask that which your personal life is in. There is very little that our personal life is in when we pray; we spell out platitudes before God and call it prayer, but it is not prayer at all. What is my personal life really in when I come before God? Jesus has pledged His honor that everything I ask with the blood of my life in, I shall have. No false emotion is necessary, we have not to conjure up petitions, they well up. The "greater works" are done by prayer because prayer is the exercise of the essential character of the life of God in us. Prayer is not meant to develop us naturally, it is meant to give the life of the Son of God in us a chance to develop that the natural order may be transfigured into the spiritual.

Moral Devotion to the Sovereign Will

". . . and the life which I now live in the flesh I live by faith in the Son of God, who loved me and gave Himself for me."

The gospel of Jesus always forces an issue of will. Do I accept God's verdict on sin in the death of Christ, namely, death? Do I want to be so identified with the death of Jesus that I am spoiled for everything saving Himself? The great privilege of discipleship is that I can sign on under His cross—and that means death to sin.

Sovereign Preference

"For to me, to live is Christ . . ." (Phil. 1:21).

Love is literally the sovereign preference of my person for another person, and Jesus says that spiritually that preference must be for Himself. When Paul said, "For to me, to live is Christ," he did not mean that he did not live for anything else but that the dominant note, the great consuming passion underneath everything, was his love for Jesus Christ—it explained everything he did. We are not always conscious of the sovereign preference, but a crisis will reveal it. So many make the blunder of mistaking the ecstasy of the first introduction into the kingdom of God for the purpose of God in getting them there; the purpose of God for us is that we realize what the death of Christ meant for *us*. When we tell God that we want at all costs to be identified with the death of Jesus Christ, at that instant a supernatural identification with His death takes place, and we know with a knowledge that passes knowledge that our "old man" is crucified with Christ, and we prove it for ever after by the amazing ease with which the supernatural life of God in us enables us to do His will. That is why the bedrock of Christianity is personal, passionate devotion to the Lord Jesus.

Sacred Presence

"And lo, I am with you always, even to the end of the age" (Matt. 28:20).

On the threshold of every new experience of life we are conscious of it, and this is true in regard to our life with God. When we are born from above we are conscious of God until we get into the life of God, then we are no longer conscious of Him because our life is "hidden with Christ in God." "I don't feel God's presence," you say; how can you when you are in God and God is in you? By asking God to give you "feelings" you are pressing back to the entrance into life again.

The moral honor of a saint is to recognize that "Christ touches us more deeply than our pain or our guilt." It is a question of the inner life between myself and God. If I am set on my own holiness, I become a traitor to Jesus. The note of the Christian life is abandonment to Jesus Christ. That life is not a hole-and-corner business whereby I look after my own speckless whiteness, afraid to do this and that, afraid to go anywhere in case I get soiled. The whole life is summed up in a passionate absorbing devotion to Jesus and the realization of His presence.

The Sublime Passion

"For I determined not to know anything among you except Jesus Christ and Him crucified" (1 Cor. 2:2).

The word "passion" has come down in the world; with us it usually means something from which human nature suffers. Passion is really the transfiguration of human plod and perseverance and patience; and when we use the word "passion" in connection with our Lord, we refer to the whole climax of His personality flashing out in an extraordinary manner, exhibiting His patience and His power and the whole personality of His life. Paul's supreme passion was for Jesus Christ. When once the Holy Spirit has come in, the thought of sacrifice never occurs to a saint because sacrifice is the love passion of the Holy Spirit. Christianity is not devotion to a cause or to a set of principles, but devotion to a person, and the great watchword of a Christian is not a passion for souls, but a passion for Christ.

YEARNING TO RECOVER GOD

Genesis 28:10–22

Jacob was a man who could dream and wait, and that is the essential nature of a true religious life. We are not all excellent supermen, walking the earth with unsullied tread; a good many of us are "Jacobs," as mean and subtle as can be; yet Jacob is the man who had the vision, and he is taken as the type of the ancient people of God. Jacob was the man to whom God appeared, and whom God altered. "Jacob have I loved." Esau is the home of all the natural vices and virtues. Perfectly contented with being once born, he does not need God, he is happy and healthy and a delight to meet; Jacob was the opposite. God loves the man who needs Him.

The Disposition of Self-Assertion

"Then Jacob made a vow, saying, 'If God will be with me, and keep me in this way that I am going . . . then the LORD shall be my God . . . and of all that You give me I will surely give a tenth to You'" (Gen. 28:20–22).

Our true character comes out in the way we pray. This is an assertive natural prayer, there is nothing noble or fine about it. All Jacob's prayers are selfish, self-assertive, and self-centered; he cares for little else outside himself. It is this kind of thing that puts Jacob where we live. A carnal will cannot rule a corrupt heart. That is the first big lesson in spiritual life. The word "carnal" is used by Paul of a religious man, never of an irreligious one. The carnal mind is the result of the Spirit of God being in a man but who has not quite yielded to Him— "For the flesh lusts against the Spirit, and the Spirit against the flesh; and these are contrary to one another, so that you do not do the things that you wish" (Gal. 5:17). It is "enmity against God." Instead of the Spirit of God bringing you peace and joy and delight, as the shallow evangelist too often puts it, His incoming has brought disturbance. In some ways you were better off before than you are now; the incoming of the Spirit of God has brought another standard and outlook, it upsets a man. "Do not think that I came to bring peace on earth. I did not come to bring peace but a sword" (Matt. 10:34). The natural pagan, a man whose word is as good as his bond, a moral and upright man, is more delightful to meet than the Christian who has enough of the Spirit of God to spoil his sin but not enough to deliver him from it.

Self-assertion is an indication that there is a struggle going on and we have to decide who is going to rule. We rarely take the standard of the Christian life laid down in the New Testament, namely, Jesus Christ; we make excuses. If I am yearning to recover God I have to come to the place where this disposition of self-assertion is located in me. One of the reasons we lose fellowship with God is that we will explain and vindicate ourselves; we will not let God hunt through us and chase out the interests of self-will and self-assertion. We are spiritual "Jacobs," men wrestling with God in prayer; to wrestle *before* God is another matter. Jacob tried to break the neck of God's answer to his prayer, and he limped all the rest of his life because of the struggle. "If God will give me what I want, I will do this thing." We cannot go on spiritually if we are self-assertive.

The Dreaming of Supreme Apprehension

"Then he dreamed, and behold, a ladder was set up on the earth, and its top reached to heaven; and there the angels of God were ascending and descending on it" (Gen. 28:12).

If the vision had come to a man like Joseph or Daniel, fine unsullied men of God, we should not have been surprised, but the vision came to a mean man. The dream was a pre-incarnation vision of God, symbolizing that communication between God and man is open, there is no break now. (John 1:51, "And He said to him, 'Most assuredly, I say to you, hereafter you shall see heaven open, and the angels of God ascending and descending upon the Son of Man.'") The only being in whom that ever took place was Jesus Christ, and He claims that He can put us where we can have the vision fulfilled in our own lives. Never say that God intends man to have a domain of dreaming, having mighty visions of God, and living an actual life that is dead to God at the same time. Jesus Christ claims that He can put into us the thing that connects the two. It is a great thing to be able to dream; it would be awful never to be touched by anything higher than the sordid. When we feel our deadness the consolation is that this vision came to Jacob. God transformed Jacob into "Israel," indicating one who strives with God. When a man is born again of the Spirit of God he has the nature of Jesus Christ imparted to him. If we are yearning to recover God, what we need is to get to the point of deciding against the self-assertiveness of our own hearts, and letting God teach us how to pay the price of our dreams.

The Devotion of Spiritual Aspiration

"And he called the name of that place Bethel" (Gen. 28:19).

Jacob could dream and wait; the biggest test is to wait. The difference between lust and love comes just here. Lust is—I must have it at once. Love can wait. Lust makes me impulsively impatient, I want to take shortcuts and do things right off. Love can wait endlessly. If I have ever seen God and been touched by Him and the Spirit of God has entered into me, I am willing to wait for Him; I wait in the certainty that He will come. The difference between a spiritual man and a man who is not spiritual is just in this power to wait. The best illustration of waiting upon God is that of a child at his mother's breast. We draw our nourishment from no one but God. The test of the strength of spiritual aspiration is—will I wait for God like that? Do I believe Jesus Christ can turn me into His disciple if I let Him have His way? Then I will wait for Him, and "hang in" until He does it.

In this way we may become a sacrament of the love of God. "Sacrament" means the real presence of God coming through the common elements. A great point in the sacramental teaching of the New Testament is that God brings His real presence through the common elements of friendship, and air, and sea, and sky. Very few of us see it. It is only when we develop in spiritual devotion to Jesus Christ that we begin to detect Him in our friendships, in our ordinary eating and drinking. The ecclesiastical doctrine of the sacraments with too many of us confines it to a particular thing, and we do not scent that it is a symbol of all life that is "hidden with Christ in God." Jesus Christ teaches that He can come to us through anything, and the great sign of a Christian man is that he finds God in ordinary ways and days, and partakes of the sacrament of His presence here.

SPIRITUAL INEFFICIENCY

"If you know these things, happy are you if you do them"
(John 13:17).

That is the big test in spiritual life. Most of us are spiritually inefficient because we cannot do certain things and remain spiritual. We can be spiritual in prayer meetings, in congenial spiritual society, in what is known as Christian work, but we cannot be spiritual in drudgery. We are all capable of being spiritual sluggards; if we live a sequestered life and continually don't do what we ought to do, we can develop a spiritual life, but in actual things we are easily knocked out. We are trying to develop a life that is sanctified and holy but it is spiritually inefficient—it cannot wash feet, it cannot do secular things without being tainted. Spiritual means *real*, and the only type of spiritual life is the life of our Lord Himself; there was no sacred and secular in His life, it was all real. Jesus Christ did secular things and was God incarnate in doing them. "After that, He poured water into a basin, and began to wash the disciples' feet, and to wipe them with the towel with which He was girded." If Christianity means anything, it means that He can produce that kind of life in us.

We may know all this, but, says Jesus that you are only happy if you really do it. Very few of us are blessed; we lose the blessing as soon as we have to wash feet, and all that that symbolizes. It takes God incarnate to do ordinary drudgery and maintain blessedness. The great marvel of the incarnation is just here.

Expression and Experience (Matt. 7:21–22)

"Not everyone who says to Me, 'Lord, Lord,' shall enter the kingdom of heaven, but he who does the will of My Father in heaven" (Matt. 7:21).

It is not sufficient to have an experience. If all I can do is to preach and recount the experiences God has given me, it is dangerously insufficient. Unless my life is the exact expression of the life of Jesus Christ, I am an abortion, an illegitimate. Experience must be worked out into expression; the expression is a strong family likeness to Jesus, and its mark is found in the secular life, not in the sequestered life. Our Lord Himself is the one standard, and to the people of His day He seemed unutterably secular.

Jesus Christ is infinitely bigger than any of my experiences, but if in my experiences I am coming to know Him better, then the expression will come out in the life, and its sign is the fruit of the Spirit—"love, joy, peace . . . ." The fruit of the Spirit is the exact expression of the disposition of Jesus. We cannot pretend to have the fruit of the Spirit if we have not; we cannot be hypocritical over it. Expression is always unconscious. "His name shall be in their foreheads"—where everyone can see it saving the man himself. We test men spiritually by the fact that they preach the gospel, that they cast out demons, that they have an experience of these things. There are many who have these experiences, and yet Jesus said He will say of such—"I never knew you; depart from Me, you who practice lawlessness!" The man who is "of Me," says

Jesus, is the man who is an exact expression of "your Father in heaven" (Matt. 5:45).

Energy and Enchantment (Acts 1:6–8)

"But you shall receive power when the Holy Spirit has come upon you; and you shall be witnesses to Me . . ." (Acts 1:8).

It is quite possible to be enchanted with Jesus Christ and with His truth and yet never to be changed by it. The disciples are enchanted; their Lord is risen from the dead and He is telling them wonderful things about His kingdom; they are enthralled, enamored, then Jesus suddenly brings them down to earth by saying, "It is not for you to know times or sea' sons . . . . But you shall receive power . . . , and you shall be witnesses to Me." Literally, "the Holy Spirit coming upon you will make you witnesses unto Me, not witnesses of what I can do, not recorders of what you have experienced, but witnesses who are a satisfaction to Me." The baptism of the Holy Spirit is usually illustrated by the fact that "and that day about three thousand souls were added to them." That was a manifestation of the power of God, but it was when the apostles were per' secuted and scattered, that the real energy of the Holy Spirit showed itself. Men "realized that they had been with Jesus." A witness is not one who is entranced by Jesus, by the revelation He gives, by what He has done; but one who has received the energy Jesus Himself had, and is become a witness that pleases Him, wherever he is placed, whatever he is doing, whether he is known or unknown. The energy in him is the very energy of the Holy Spirit, and the expression of it in life makes a witness that satisfies Jesus Christ.

There is a real peril in being enchanted but unchanged. I may be enchanted by the truth Jesus presents, but when it comes to my life being marked in all its secular details with the disposition of the Holy Spirit, then I am out of it; I prove spiritually inefficient, of no worth at all to Jesus Christ. Experiences are good, enchantment is good, but it all makes for spiritual inefficiency unless the experience is turned into the expression of a strong family likeness to Jesus, and the enchantment is transformed into the energy of the Holy Spirit.

Epistles and Experts (2 Cor. 3:1–6)

"You are our epistle written in our hearts, known and read by all men" (2 Cor. 3:2).

An "epistle of Christ" means a reincarnation of Jesus. Thank God for experiences, for the power to be enchanted, but this is the thing that tells—"Christ in you." I may be able to expound the Word of God, I may be an expert in a great many things, but unless my experience shows in expression a strong family likeness to Jesus, it is making me spiritually inefficient; I may be enchanted with the truth, but unless my enchantment is transformed into the energy which bears the mark of the disposition of Jesus, it is making for spiritual inefficiency. I may be expert in the knowledge of Scripture and expert in Christian work, but if all this is not turning me into an epistle in which men can read "Jesus," it is making for spiritual inefficiency. Is the expression in my life more and more the expression of the indwelling Holy Spirit? Is my energy the energy that comes direct from my risen Lord? Is my life an epistle that spells only one thing—God? Is the dominating interest in my life God? Have I any other dominating interest? If I have, then none of my energy or expert knowledge is telling in the tiniest degree for Jesus.

The spiritual life can never be lived in religious meetings, it can only be lived on sordid earth, where Jesus lived, among the things that make human life what it is. "If I then, your Lord and Teacher, have washed your feet, you also ought to wash one another's feet." That is the only way we can justify what we say we have experienced of the grace of God. Our visions of God, our enchantment of His power, our expert knowledge of Him, will all amount to nothing unless it is made manifest in our actual life.

WITH GOD AT THE FRONT

"Behold, we are going up to Jerusalem" (Luke 18:31).

Jerusalem stands in the life of our Lord for the place where He reached the full climax of God's will. That will was the one dominating interest all through His life, and the things He met on the way, joy or sorrow, success or failure, never deterred Him from His purpose; He steadfastly went up to Jerusalem. The same thing is true of us, there is one definite aim in every Christian life, and that aim is not ours, it is God's. In our natural life our ambitions are our own. In the Christian life we have no aim of our own, and God's aim looks like missing the mark because we are too short-sighted to see what He is aiming at. The great thing to remember is that we go up to Jerusalem to fulfill God's purpose, not our own.

The Big Compelling of God

"Then He took the twelve aside" (Luke 18:31).

One needs to dwell on this aspect of the big compelling of God. There is so much talk about our decision for Christ, our determination to be Christians, our decisions for this and for that. When we come to the New Testament we find that the other aspect, God's choosing of us, is the one that is brought out the oftenest. "You did not choose Me, but I chose you . . ."

(John 15:16). We are not taken up into conscious agreement with God's purpose, we are taken up into His purpose without any consciousness on our part at all; we have no conception of what God is aiming at, and it gets more and more vague as we go on. At the beginning of our Christian life we have our own particular notions as to what God's purpose is—we are meant to go here or there; or God has called us to do this or that piece of work. We go and do the thing and still we find the big compelling of God remains. The majority of the work we do is so much scaffolding to further the purpose of the big compelling of God. "Then He took the twelve aside." He takes us all the time; there is more than we have got at, something we have not seen.

As we go on in the Christian life it gets simpler, for the very reason that we get less inclined to say, "Now, why did God allow this and that?" When the Holy Spirit of God enters into a man, it is the same Spirit that was in Jesus Christ. "God so loved *the world* . . ." and the Holy Spirit implants the same kind of love in our hearts. The thing that compels us to take the line we do is never discernible to ourselves, it is symbolized spiritually by this compelling. "Then He took the twelve aside and said to them, 'Behold, we are going up to Jerusalem.'" How perplexing it must have sounded to them!

The main thing about Christianity is not the work we do, but the relationship we maintain. The only things God asks us to look after are the atmosphere of our life and our relationships, these are the only things that preserve us from priggishness, from impertinence, and from worry, and it is these things that are assailed all through.

As soon as I complain and say, "Why does God allow this?" I am not only useless but dangerous, I am taken up with compelling God. It is rarely the big compellings of God that get hold of us in our prayers, instead we tell God what He should do, we tell Him that men are being lost and that He ought to save them. This is a terrific charge against God, it means that He must be asleep. When God gets me to realize that I am being taken up into *His* enterprises, then I get rest of soul, I am free for my twenty-four hours. Whenever I have an important fuss on, I have no room for God; I am not being taken by God, I have an aim and purpose of my own. In laying down His conditions for discipleship in Luke 14:26–33, our Lord implies, "the only men I will use in My enterprises, are those of whom I have taken charge." The illustration is that of a soldier who has forsaken all to fight. I am not out for my own end and purpose; the great campaign is God's, not mine. What man gives his life for his king and country only? Not one man. That is a very shallow watchword. Every man who has given his life has given it for something infinitely bigger; there is something entirely other and different behind. We may try to serve our own ends, but underneath is the compelling of another purpose, and it is to be hoped that the empire to which we belong is seeing the bigger purpose.

How can I know my way when it is God who is planning it out for me? How can I understand the architect's plan? To have a purpose of my own will destroy the simplicity and the gaiety of a child of God, and the leisureliness which enables me to help other people. When a man is taken up into the big compellings of God, God is responsible. Amid all the terrors of war there is one remarkable thing, and that is, apart from grousings, the spirit of freedom and gaiety in the very bondage of it. The man who joins up has to have his individuality trampled on so that his personality might be merged into the personality of his regiment; he ceases to be of any account at all as an individual, responsibility is not his any longer.

The Brave Comradeship of God

"Behold, we are going up to Jerusalem."

The bravery of God in trusting us! It is a tremendously risky thing to do, it looks as if all the odds were against Him. The majority of us don't bother much about Him, and yet He deliberately stakes all He has on us, He stands by and lets the world, the flesh, and the devil do their worst, confident we will come out all right. All our Lord succeeded in doing during His life on earth was to gather together a group of fishermen—the whole church of God and the enterprise of our Lord on earth in a fishing boat!

We say, "It seems out of all proportion that God should choose me—I am of no value"; the reason He chooses us is that we are not of any value. It is folly to think that because a man has natural ability, he must make a good Christian. People with the best natural equipment may make the worst disciples because they will "boss" themselves. It is not a question of our equipment, but of our poverty; not what we bring with us, but what He puts in us; not our natural virtues, our strength of character, our knowledge, our experience; all that is of no avail in this matter; the only thing that is of avail is that we are taken up into the big compelling of God and made His comrade (1 Cor. 1:26–28). His comradeship is made out of men who know their poverty. God can do nothing with the men who think they will be of use to Him. "If we can only add him to our cause"—that is where the competition comes in. We are not out for our cause at all as Christians, we are out for the cause of God, which can never be our cause. It is not that God is on our side, we must see that we are on God's side, which is a different matter. We do not know what God is after, but we have to maintain our relationship to Him whatever happens. Never allow anything to injure your relationship to God, cut it out at once; if you are getting out of touch with God, take time and get it right.

The Baffling Call of God

". . . and all things that are written by the prophets concern-ing the Son of Man will be accomplished" (Luke 18:31).

God called Jesus Christ to unmitigated disaster; Jesus Christ called His disciples to come and see Him put to death; He led every one of those disciples to the place where their hearts broke. The whole thing was an absolute failure from every standpoint but God's, and yet the thing that was the biggest failure from man's standpoint was the ultimate triumph from God's, because God's purpose was not man's.

In our own lives there comes the baffling call of God. "Let us go over to the other side," Jesus said to His disciples; they obeyed, but as soon as they got into the boat there arose a great storm of wind and there was a squall that nearly drowned them. The call of God cannot be stated explicitly, it is implicit. The call of God is like the call of the sea, no one hears it but the man who has the nature of the sea in him. You cannot state definitely what the call of God is to; it is to be in comradeship with God for His own purposes, and the test of faith is to believe God knows what He is after. The fact that history fulfills prophecy is a small matter compared to our mainte-nance of a right relationship to God who is working out His purposes. The things that happen do not happen by chance at all, they happen entirely in the decrees of God.

To be "with God at the front" means the continual mainte-nance of our relationship to Him. If I maintain communion with God and recognize that He is taking me up into His purposes, I will no longer try to find out what those purposes are. The war has hit every kind of cause there is, but that does not mean it has hit God. Behind it all are the big compellings of God, and in it we see the brave comradeship of God. If God has been brave enough to trust me, surely it is up to me not to let Him down, but to "hang in." You say, "God has been very unwise to choose me because there is nothing in me." As long as there is something in you He cannot choose you, because you have ends of your own to serve; but if you have let Him bring you to the end of your self-sufficiency, then He can choose you to go with Him to Jerusalem, and that means the fulfillment of His purposes which He does not discuss with you at all. We go on with Him, and in the final wind-up the glory of God will be manifested before our eyes. No wonder our way is inscrutable! "There's a divinity that shapes our ends"; we may take what ways we like, but behind them come the big compellings of God. The Christian is one who trusts the wisdom of God, not his own wits. The astute mind behind the saint's life is the mind of God, not his own mind.

Aotea Home, 10 June 1917

THE UNSPEAKABLE WONDER

In new birth God does three impossible things, impossible, that is, from the rational standpoint. The first is to make a man's past as though it had never been; the second, to make a man all over again; and the third, to make a man as certain of God as God is of Himself. New birth does not mean merely salvation from hell, but something more radical, something which tells in a man's actual life.

Of the Road Back to Yesterday

"So I will restore to you the years that the swarming locust has eaten, the crawling locust, the consuming locust, and the chewing locust, My great army which I sent among you" (Joel 2:25).

Through the redemption God undertakes to deal with a man's past, and He does it in two ways: by forgiving him, and by making the past a wonderful culture for the future. The forgiveness of God is a bigger miracle than we are apt to think. It is impossible for a human being to forgive; and it is because this is not realized that we fail to understand that the forgive-ness of God is a miracle of divine grace. Do I really believe that God cannot, dare not, must not forgive me my sin without its being atoned for? If God were to forgive me my sin without its being atoned for, I should have a greater sense of justice than God. It is not that God says in effect, "I will pay no more attention to what you have done." When God forgives a man, He not only alters him but transmutes what he has already done. Forgiveness does not mean merely that I am saved from sin and made right for heaven; forgiveness means that I am forgiven into a recreated relationship to God.

Do I believe that God can deal with my "yesterday," and make it as though it had never been? I either do not believe He can, or I do not want Him to. Forgiveness, which is so easy for us to accept, cost God the agony of Calvary. When Jesus Christ says, "Sin no more," He conveys the power that enables a man not to sin any more, and that power comes by right of what He did on the cross. That is the unspeakable wonder of the forgiveness of God. Today men do not bank on what Jesus Christ can do, or on the miraculous power of God; they only look at things from their side—"I should like to be a man or a woman after God's heart, but look at the mountain of my past that is in the way." God has promised to do the thing, which looked at from the basis of our own reason, cannot be done. If a man will commit his "yesterday" to God, make it irrevocable, and bank in confidence on what Jesus Christ has done, he will know what is meant by spiritual mirth—"Then our mouth was filled with laughter, and our tongue with singing." Very few of us get there because we do not believe Jesus Christ means what He says. "It is impossible! Can Jesus Christ re-make me, with my meanness and my criminality; remake not only my actual life, but my mind and my dreams?" Jesus said, "With God all things are possible." The reason God cannot do it for us is because of our unbelief; it is not that God *won't* do it if we do not believe, but that our commitment to Him is part of the essential relationship.

Of the Renewal of Youth

"But Jesus said, 'Let the little children come to Me, and do not forbid them; for of such is the kingdom of heaven'" (Matt. 19:14).

Jesus Christ uses the child-spirit as a touchstone for the character of a disciple. He did not put up a child before His disciples as an ideal, but as an expression of the simple-hearted life they would live when they were born again. The life of a little child is expectant, full of wonder, and free from self-consciousness, and Jesus said, "Unless you are converted and become as little children, you will by no means enter the kingdom of heaven." We cannot enter into the kingdom of heaven head first. How many of us thought about how we should live before we were born? Why, none. But numbers of people try to think of how to live as Christians before they are born again. "Do not marvel that I said to you, 'You must be born again,'" that is, become as little children, with openhearted, unprejudiced minds in relation to God. There is a marvelous rejuvenescence once we let God have His way. The most seriously minded Christian is the one who has just become a Christian; the mature saint is just like a young child, absolutely simple, and joyful and gay. Read the Sermon on the Mount— "Do not worry," (that is, have no care) "about your life." The word "care" has within it the idea of something that buffets. The Christianity of Jesus Christ refuses to be careworn. Our Lord is indicating that we have to be carefully careless about everything saving our relationship to Him. Fuss is always a sign of fever. A great many people mistake perspiration in service for inspiration in devotion. The characteristic of a man who has come to God is that you cannot get him to take anyone seriously but God.

Spiritually beware of anything that takes the wonder out of life and makes you take a prosaic attitude; when you lose wonder, you lose life. The Spirit of God creates the intuitions of a child in a man and keeps him in touch with the elemental and real, and the miracle of Christianity is that a man can be made young in heart and mind and spirit.

Of the Repleteness of "Yes"

"And in that day you will ask Me nothing. Most assuredly, I say to you, whatever you ask the Father in My name He will give you" (John 16:23).

When once we strike the "everlasting yes," there is something positive all through our life. So many of us never get beyond the "everlasting no"; there is a nebulous "knockoutedness" about us—"Oh yes, I will pray, but I know what the answer will be." When we come to the repleteness of "yes," the moral miracle God works in us is that we ask only what is exactly in accordance with God's nature, and the repleteness begins, the fullness and satisfaction of the "everlasting yes." "And in that day you will ask Me nothing." That does not mean that God will give us everything we ask for, but that God can do with us now exactly what He likes. We have no business to tell God we cannot stand any more; God ought to be at liberty to do with us what He chooses, as He did with His own Son. Then whatever happens our life will be full of joy.

Anyone who has not found the road back to yesterday, who has not experienced the renewal of youth, and the repleteness of the "everlasting yes," has farther to go. The unspeakable wonder is that God undertakes to do all this with the human stuff of which we are made. The emphasis put on the nobility of man is largely a matter of fiction. Men and women are men and women, and it is absurd to pretend they are either better or worse than they are. Most of us begin by demanding perfect justice and nobility and generosity from other people, then we see their defects and become bitter and cynical. Jesus Christ never trusted human nature, yet He was never cynical, never in despair about any man, because He trusted absolutely in what the grace of God could do in human nature.

ACQUAINTANCE WITH GRIEF

"But this is your hour, and the power of darkness" (Luke 22:53).

There are times when God distinctly allows the wrong thing to have its hour; every one of us more or less has had this experience in his own life. We are not "acquainted with grief" in the way our Lord was; we endure it, we get through the thing, but we do not get intimate with anything in it.

Reconciling One's Self to the Fact of Sin

The climax of sin is that it crucified Jesus Christ. When we begin our life we do not reconcile ourselves to the fact of sin; we take a rational view of life and say that a man by looking after his own instincts, educating himself, controlling the ape and the tiger in him, can produce that life which will slowly evolve into the life of God. But as we go on we find there is something that we have not taken into consideration, namely, sin, and it upsets all our calculations. Sin has made the basis of things not rational, but wild. Take the life of Jesus Christ, it seems an anticlimax that the end of that life should be a tragedy, yet it did end that way. All He succeeded in doing was to gather together a handful of fishermen as disciples, one of whom betrayed Him, another of whom denied Him, and all of whom "forsook Him and fled."

We do not get reconciled to the fact of sin; we do not think it should be there. Take the attitude of men's minds with regard to this war; they said that it was impossible for war to be, it was out of all reason to imagine that Christian nations would tear one another to pieces, yet that is what is actually happening. To be "acquainted with grief" and to reconcile one's self to the fact of sin is the biggest factor in our life and outlook. Men say if God had ordered the world otherwise, there would be no sin; Jesus Christ would not have been killed, men would not be at war; but men are at war, and sin is, and everywhere Jesus Christ's words are proving true: "This is your hour, and the power of darkness." There is a time when the hour of sin is unhindered, it is deliberate and emphatic and clear. I have to recognize that sin is a fact, not a defect; it is red-handed mutiny against God, and acquaintance with the grief of it means that unless I withstand it to the death, it will withstand me to the death. If sin rules in me, the life of God will be killed in me; if God rules in me, sin will be killed in me. There is no possible ultimate but that.

In our mental outlook we have to reconcile ourselves to the fact that sin is the only explanation as to why Jesus Christ came, the only explanation of the grief and the sorrow that there is in life. There may be a great deal that is pathetic in a man's condition, but there is also a lot that is bad and wrong. There is the downright spiteful thing, as wrong as wrong can be, without a strand of good in it, in you and in me and in other people by nature, and we have to reconcile ourselves to the fact that there is sin. That does not mean that we compromise with sin, it means that we face the fact that it is there. If we try to estimate ourselves or to estimate human history and ignore sin, we are not reconciling ourselves to the fact of sin;

we are not becoming acquainted with the grief produced by sin, and unless we do we shall never understand why Jesus Christ came as He did, and why He said, "this is your hour, and the power of darkness."

At present in the history of the world it is the hour and the power of darkness. During the war some of the biggest intellectual juggling tricks have been performed trying to make out that war is a good thing; war is the most damnably bad thing. Because God overrules a thing and brings good out of it does not mean that in itself that thing is a good thing. We have not been getting "acquainted with grief," we have tried to juggle with the cause of it. If the war has made me reconcile myself with the fact that there is sin in human beings, I shall no longer go with my head in the clouds, or hidden in the sand like an ostrich, but I shall be willing to face facts as they are.

It is not being reconciled to the fact of sin that produces all the disasters in life. We talk about noble human nature, selfsacrifice, and platonic friendship—all unmitigated nonsense. Unless we recognize the fact of sin, there is something that will laugh and spit in the face of every ideal we have. Unless we reconcile ourselves to the fact that there will come a time when the power of darkness will have its own way, and that by God's permission, we will compromise with that power when its hour comes. If we refuse to take the fact of sin into our calculation, refuse to agree that a base impulse runs through men, that there is such a thing as vice and selfseeking, when our hour of darkness strikes, instead of being acquainted with sin and the grief of it, we will compromise straightaway and say there is no use battling against it. To be "acquainted with grief" and with the fact of sin means that I will endure to the crack of doom, but will never compromise with it. The man who accepts salvation from Jesus Christ recognizes the fact of sin, he does not ignore it. Thereafter he will not demand too much of human beings.

Receiving One's Self in the Fires of Sorrow

"Now My soul is troubled, and what shall I say? 'Father, save Me from this hour'. But for this purpose I came to this hour" (John 12:27).

Jesus Christ is asking God to save Him *out of* the hour, not *from* it. All through, that is the inner attitude of Jesus Christ, He received Himself in the fires of sorrow; it was never, "Do not let the sorrow come." That is the opposite of what we do, we pray, "Oh, Lord, don't let this or that happen to me"; consequently all kinds of damaging and blasphemous things are said about answers to prayer. You hear of one man who has gone safely through battles, and friends tell him it is in answer to prayer; does that mean that the prayers for the men who have gone under have not been answered? We have to remember that the hour of darkness will come in every life. It is not that we are saved from the hour of sorrow, but that we are delivered in it. "But you are those who have continued with Me in My trials" (Luke 22:28). Our Lord said He prayed for Peter, not that Satan should not sift him, but that his faith should not fail. The attitude of Jesus Christ Himself to the coming sorrows and difficulties was not to ask that they might be prevented, but that He might be saved out of them.

People say there ought to be no sorrow; but the fact remains that there *is* sorrow, there is not one family just now without its sorrow, and we have to learn to receive ourselves in its fires. If we try to evade sorrow and refuse to lay our account with it, we are foolish, for sorrow is one of the biggest facts in life, and there is no use saying it ought not to be, it is. It is ridiculous to say things ought not to be when they are. A man who wants to find an explanation of why things are as they are is an intellectual lunatic. There is nothing gained by saying, "Why should there be sin and sorrow and suffering?" They *are*; it is not for me to find out why God made what I am pleased to consider a mistake; I have to find out what to do in regard to it all.

Jesus Christ's attitude is that I have to receive myself in the fires of sorrow. It is never those who go through suffering who are in doubt, but those who watch them suffer. In the majority of cases those who have gone through the sorrow have received their "self" in its fires. That is not the same as saying that they have been made better by it; sorrow does not necessarily make a man better; sorrow burns up a great amount of unnecessary shallowness, it gives me my self, or it destroys me. If a man becomes acquainted with sorrow, the gift it presents him with is his self.

We cannot receive ourselves in success, we lose our heads; we cannot receive ourselves in monotony, we grouse; the only way we can find ourselves is in the fires of sorrow. Why it should be so I do not know, but that it is so is true not only in Scripture, but in human life. The people who have gone through the fires of sorrow in this war have not become skeptical of God; it is those who have watched others going through it who have become bitter. The letters written by friends to friends during the calamitous disasters and fires of sorrow in this war in which they have discovered themselves will be most marvelous to read after the war is over.

Recognizing One's Self in the Fullness of Sanctity

"And for their sakes I sanctify Myself" (John 17:19).

Jesus Christ was holy; then why did He say, "I sanctify Myself"? Jesus Christ took his holy self and deliberately gave it to God to do what He liked with. The spiritual order of Jesus Christ in my life is that I take what God has given me and give it back to Him; that is the essence of worship. The purpose of salvation and sanctification is that we may be made broken bread and poured out wine for others as Jesus Christ was made broken bread and poured out wine for us. When we recognize God's purpose we hand ourselves back to God to do what He likes with. He may put me in the front of things, or He may put me on the shelf if He wants to. I separate the holy thing God has created to the holy God.

To come back to our personal relationships. Have we made allowance there for the hour and the power of darkness, or do we take the recognition of ourselves that misses it out? In our own bodily relationships, in our friendships, do we reconcile ourselves to the fact that there is sin? If not, we will be caught round the next corner of the high-road and begin to compromise with it. If we recognize that sin is there we will not make that mistake. "Yes, I see what that means and where it would lead me." Always beware of a friendship, or of a religion, or of a personal estimate of things that does not reconcile itself to the fact of sin; that is the way all the disasters in human friendships and in human loves begin, and where the compromises start. Jesus Christ never trusted human nature, but He was never cynical, He trusted absolutely what He could do for human nature. The safeguarded man or woman is the pure man or woman. No man or woman has any right to be innocent. God demands of men and women that they be pure and virtuous. Innocence is the characteristic of a child, but it is an ignorant and blameworthy thing for a man or woman not to be reconciled to the fact that there is sin. To be forewarned is to be forearmed. Instead of the recognition of sin destroying the basis of friendship, it establishes a mutual regard founded on the fact that the basis of life is tragedy.

Again, in sorrow—you have some personal grief, it may be a question of bereavement, of unrequited love, or of any of those things that bite desperately. Have you received your self out of it yet? Or are you ignoring it? It is a foolish thing to ignore the fact that you are hurt; the only thing to do is to receive yourself in the fires of the sorrow. Am I receiving myself in sorrow, or am I getting meaner and more spiteful? If I am getting sarcastic and spiteful, it is an indication that I am being sorely bitten by the fire, but am not receiving my self in its fires. The attitude of anyone watching a person going through sorrow and becoming cynical is not to condemn that one, but to realize that he is being hurt, and badly hurt. Cynicism is never the outcome of being hurt in the fires of sorrow, but of not recognizing that through the sorrow comes the chance to receive one's self.

Through the fires of suffering emerges the kind of manhood and womanhood Peter mentions in his epistle—"Therefore let those who suffer according to the will of God commit their souls to Him in doing good, as to a faithful Creator." You always know the person who has been through the fires of sorrow and has received himself; you never smell the fire on him, and you are certain you can go to him when you are in trouble. It is not the man with the signs of sorrow on him who is helpful, but the one who has gone through the fires and received himself; he is delivered from the small side of himself, and has ample leisure for others. The one who has not been through the fires of sorrow has no time for you and is inclined to be contemptuous and impatient. If I have received myself in the fire of sorrow, then I am good stuff for other people in the same condition.

What standard have I for the outcome of my life? The standard of Jesus Christ is that I may be perfect as my Father in heaven is perfect. Jesus Christ is not after making a fine character or a virtuous man; those are ingredients to another end: His end is that we may be children of our Father in heaven. The best way to know whether I am recognizing myself in the fullness of sanctity is to watch how I behave towards the mean folks who come around. If I am learning to behave to them as God behaved to me in Jesus Christ, then I am all right; but if I have no time for them, it means that I am growing meaner and more selfish. Our Father is kind to the unthankful, to the mean. He tells us to be the same. The idea of sanctity is that we must be perfect in these relationships in life.

ENTHUSIASTIC AND CAPABLE

The Rejoicing Inspiration of Life

"Be filled with the Spirit" (Eph. 5:18).

We think that sobriety and capability go together, but it is not always so. A man may be sober and incapable as well as drunk and incapable. Paul warns against the enthusiasm according to wine, but he says we have no business to be nondescript, negative people, drunk neither one way nor the other; we must be enthusiastic. In other words, "Be being filled." The teaching of the New Testament presents the passion of life. Stoicism has come so much into the idea of the Christian life that we imagine the stoic is the best type of Christian; but just where stoicism seems most like Christianity it is most adverse. A stoic overcomes the world by passionlessness, by eviscerating all personal interest out of life until he is a mere submissive recording machine. Christianity overcomes the world by passion, not by passionlessness. Passion is usually taken to mean something from which human nature suffers; in reality it stands for endurance and high enthusiasm, a radiant intensity of life, life at the highest pitch all the time without any reaction. That is what Paul means by being filled.

If a grain of radium is kept in a box the light will remain for a while after the radium is removed, but it becomes imperceptibly fainter, and at last fades away. The spiritual life of many Christians is like that; it is borrowed and not real; for a time it looks magnificent, but after a while it wilts clean out because it has no life in itself, it has to be kept alive by meetings and conventions.

The Radiant Intensity of Life

"These things I have spoken to you . . . that your joy may be full" (John 15:11).

The emphasis of the New Testament is on joy, not on happiness. The one thing about the apostle Paul that staggered his contemporaries was his unaccountable gaiety of spirit; he would not be serious over anything other than Jesus Christ. They might stone him and imprison him, but whatever they did made no difference to his buoyancy of spirit. The external character of the life of our Lord was that of radiant sociability; so much so, that the popular scandalmongering about Him was that He was "a glutton and a wine bibber, a friend of tax collectors and sinners!" The fundamental reason for our Lord's sociability was other than they knew; but His whole life was characterized with a radiant fullness, it was not an exhausted type of life. "Unless you . . . become as little children . . . ." If a little child is not full of the spontaneousness of life there is something wrong. The bounding life and restlessness is a sign of health, not of naughtiness. Jesus said, "I have come that they may have life, and that they may have it more abundantly." Be being filled with the life Jesus came to give. Men who are radiantly healthy, physically and spiritually, cannot be crushed. They are like the cedars of Lebanon, which have such superabounding vitality in their sap that they intoxicate to death any parasites that try to live on them.

The Recognized Interest of Life

"Awake, you who sleep" (Eph. 5:14).

Have I awakened into this radiance of life, the real incoming life of God? St. Augustine said he did not want to be roused out of his sleep—"I want to live in the twilight a bit longer and not be roused up to vitality just yet." Has the twilight we desired been turned into trembling? We all like the twilight in spiritual and moral matters, not the intensity of black and white, not the clear lines of demarcation—saved and unsaved. We prefer things to be hazy, winsome, and indefinite, without the clear light. When the light does come, difficulty is experienced, for when a man awakens he sees a great many things. We may feel complacent with a background of drab, but to be brought up against the white background of Jesus Christ is an immensely uncomfortable thing.

"Arise from the dead, and Christ will give you light." If you arise from the dead, Christ will shine upon you. The one thing that Jesus Christ does for a man is to make him radiant, not artificially radiant. There is nothing more irritating than the counsel, "keep smiling"; that is a counterfeit, a radiance that soon fizzles out. The joy that Jesus gives is the result of our disposition being at one with His own disposition. The Spirit of God will fill us to overflowing if we will be careful to keep in the light. We have no business to be weak in God's strength.

"See then that you walk circumspectly." We have to walk in the light "as He is in the light." Keep continually coming to the light, don't keep anything covered up. If we are filled with the life of Jesus we must walk circumspectly, keep the interest in life going, have nothing folded up. The evidence that we are being filled with the life of God is that we are not deceived about the things that spring from ourselves and the things that spring from Jesus Christ. If you have sinned, says John, confess it, keep in the light all through.

THE THROES OF THE ULTIMATE

1 Peter 1:3–9

"In this you greatly rejoice, though now for a little while, if need be, you have been grieved by various trials" (1 Pet. 1:6).

By "the ultimate" is meant here the real aim and end that God has in view. Once we get caught up into that life, Peter says, we will find there are throes in it, what we understand in physical life by "growing pains." When we think on unusual lines we get a headache because our brains are rusty. This accounts for the inevitable throes of getting at an ultimate end in our thinking. The same thing is true spiritually, no man can be virtuous without throes—without pangs and pains. The difference between Esau and Jacob lies here, that Esau was not concerned about virtue. The man who gets into the throes of a moral ultimate and determines to be something in his moral life, knows all about the pangs of producing a virtuous life. No man is born virtuous, we are born innocent; virtue is the outcome of conflict. Any man who lives a merely natural life is an animal, and he will know it himself better than anyone before long.

"Though now for a little while, if need be, you have been grieved . . . ." There is only one judge of the "need be," and that is our Father in heaven. We cannot judge what seasons are best for the natural world, nor yet for our soul's life, but whatever the seasons may be, He is bringing it all out toward one end. Peter would have us remember that there are times when we are in heaviness, when it looks as if God did not answer our prayer, as if faith had no lift about it, as if everything we ever believed in was nothing at all. Then is the time to "hang in," says Peter, remember what you saw when you had the light. No matter how manifold the temptations may be, God is producing a good thing.

The Undefiled Inheritance

"To an inheritance incorruptible and undefiled and that does not fade away, reserved in heaven for you" (1 Pet. 1:4).

". . . reserved in heaven for you." This is a great conception of the New Testament, but it is a conception lost in modern evangelism. We are so much taken up with what God wants us to be here that we have forgotten heaven. There are one or two conceptions about heaven that have to be traced back to their home to find out whether they have their root in our faith or whether they are foreign flowers. As, for instance, during this war men are producing flowers of skepticism which are not home-grown at all, but which are covers to hide the real throes of a man's mind, so there are conceptions of heaven which have not their root in Christianity. One of these is that heaven is a state and not a place; that is only a partial truth, for there cannot be a state without a place. The great New Testament conception of heaven is "here-after" without the sin, "new heavens and a new earth in which righteousness dwells"—a conception beyond us. Peter is reminding every Christian that there is an undefiled inheritance awaiting us which has never yet been realized, and that it has in it all we have ever hoped or dreamed or imagined, and a good deal more. It is always "better to come" in the Christian life until the "best of all" comes.

There is another flower abroad today which has not its root in the New Testament—the idea that when a man dies for his king and country he has thereby redeemed his soul; that is a flower which does not belong to the Christian faith. People say if a man dies in doing his duty, surely that is acceptable to God. Of course it is, but a man cannot redeem his own soul by so doing, that is God's business, and the revelation given through Jesus Christ is that the human race has been redeemed. "It is finished," and in the cross of Jesus Christ all men are condemned to salvation. That is very different from what is called Universalism. The redemption is of universal application, but human responsibility is not done away with. Universalism looks like a Christian flower, but it has not its roots in the Christian faith. Jesus Christ is most emphatic on the fact that there are possibilities of eternal damnation for the man who positively neglects or positively rejects His redemption. In John 3:19, our Lord is talking about individual lives on the experiential line. "This is the condemnation," that is, the critical moment—not the sovereign purpose of God, nor the decree of God, but the critical moment in individual experience—"that the light," Jesus Christ, "has come into the world, and men," individual men, "loved darkness," their own point of view, their own prejudices, and preconceived determinations, "rather than light." That, says Jesus, is the judgment.

This, then, is the basis of our faith. Peter says, despair of no man, and remember that there is an undefiled inheritance ahead. That is the ultimate, and we have to live in the light of it. It is a wonderful thing to see a man or woman live in the light of something you cannot see. You can always tell a man or woman who has a standard of life other than you can see; there is something that keeps them sweet when from every other consideration they ought to be sour. That is a mark of the Christian, he does not go under in the difficulties; the thing that keeps him is that he has an anchor that holds within the veil. The mainspring of a man's action is further in than you can see in his actual life and it accounts for his outlook. When a man has his anchorage in Jesus Christ and knows what is awaiting the human race—that there is a time coming when all things shall be explained fully—it keeps his spirit filled with uncrushable gaiety and joy.

The Unrelieved Rigors

"That the genuineness of your faith, being much more precious than gold that perishes, though it is tested by fire, may be found to praise, honor, and glory at the revelation of Jesus Christ" (1 Pet. 1:7).

Peter says that there are times when you won't see the vision, when you won't feel the touch of Jesus Christ, when there is no kind of inspiration at work in you, when it is all heaviness through unrelieved rigors and temptation. Jesus Christ was alone in the desert with wild beasts—the last rugged touch of human isolation. "Then the devil left Him, and behold, angels came and ministered to Him." That is the proof that you have come through the trial of your faith all right. You have no trophy, it has been a desperate time, you seem to have lost your hold on everything you can state, there has been no inspiration and no joy and you have nothing to bring away, all you can do is to dumbly "hang in" to your undefiled inheritance. The sign that you have gone through the trial rightly is that you retain your affinity with the highest. Do you feel yourself just as fond of the best as you were? Just as full of affinity with the most spiritual people when you meet them? As full of affection for those who live the highest and talk the purest? If so, you have gone grandly through.

Faith must be tried or it is not faith, faith is not mathematics nor reason. Scriptural faith is not to be illustrated by the faith we exhibit in our common sense life, it is trust in the character of one we have never seen, in the integrity of Jesus Christ, and it must be tried. "Lay up for yourselves treasures in heaven . . . for where your treasure is, there your heart will be also." You have your time of unrelieved rigor when common sense facts and your faith in Jesus Christ do not agree, and you are stepping out in the dark on His word; when you have gone through the test and are standing firm, that gives you, as it were, so many dollars in the bank, and when the next trial comes, God hands out to you a sufficient amount of your own wealth to carry you through. "Lay up for yourselves treasures in heaven," and it is the trial of faith that does it. "Oh yes, I believe God can do everything," but, *have I proved that He can do one thing*? If so, the next time the trial comes, I can not only hold myself, but someone else. It is a great thing to meet a man who believes in God, one who has not only retained his faith in God, but is continually getting a bigger faith.

There is no evidence of God outside the moral domain. The New Testament increases and educates the faith of those who know God. I do not need anyone to tell me about Jesus Christ. I know Him on the inside. It is a wonderful thing to be able to give a hand to a man who is in the turmoil, and I cannot do it by giving him platitudes. It is easy to say, "Oh yes, just trust in God." If the man sees you are not doing so yourself, it won't help him; but if he sees you are trusting God, there will come through you a tremendous assistance. When I see a person who has been through trials and who knows God, going under in some trial of his faith, I feel inclined to hang my head in shame. To see a Christian going under either in moods or in circumstances is to me a slander against Jesus Christ. It is an awful thing to see a man or woman who knows Jesus Christ begin to get sulky and dumpy under difficulties (there is a difference between this and going through the first trial of faith) begin to sink and forget the inheritance undefiled forget that the honor of Jesus Christ is at stake in His disciple. It is dishonorable, it is caddish. Buck up and face the music, get rerelated to things. It is a great thing to see physical courage, and greater still to see moral courage, but the greatest to see of all is spiritual courage, to see a man who will stand true to the integrity of Jesus Christ no matter what he is going through.

If you know a man who has a good spiritual banking account, borrow from him for all you are worth, because he will give you all you want and never look to be paid back. Here is the reason a saint goes through the things he does go through—God wants to know if He can make him good "bread" to feed other people with. The man who has gone through the crucible is going to be a tremendous support to hundreds of others.

The Unrecorded Revelation

"Whom having not seen you love. Though now you do not see Him, yet believing, you rejoice with joy inexpressible and full of glory, receiving the end of your faith—the salvation of your souls" (1 Pet. 1:8–9).

"Soul" means a great deal more than we mean when we talk about a "saved soul." "Receiving the end of your faith," the issue of your faith—the whole of your reasoning and conception of things will be completely saved, saved into the perfect light and liberty of God. If you stick steadfastly, not to your faith, but to the one who gives you the faith, there is a time coming when your whole way of being impressed, and your reasoning, will be made clear to your own satisfaction. In the meantime you have to be quiet about a good many things. You cannot stand up for Christ other than spiritually. A man slanders Jesus Christ and says, "Why does not God end the war?" and you cannot say a thing; if you do, it is nonsense. At present you have one of the hardest humiliations to stand because you have a faith that apparently in the meantime is flatly contradicted, a faith marked out by your own inconsistencies and by other people's. Peter counsels, "Now you are grieved by various trials, but hang in, remember the inheritance undefiled, look to Jesus, and you will receive the end of your faith." There is a time coming when everything that at present is a problem will be perfectly solved; in the meantime are you prepared to let men gibe at you, to let them have their immediate triumph over the matter, while you "hang in" to your grander horizon, to the very essence of Christianity, which is personal relationship to Jesus Christ? Look to Him, which means spiritual discernment, remembering it is a crime to be weak in God's strength, a crime to go under in anything when Jesus Christ is what He is. If you have a trial of faith, endure it till you get through. If you have been through trials of faith in the past, God is bringing across your path immature souls, and you have no business to despise them but rather to help them through—be to them something that has to be "sucked." "Jesus . . . knowing in Himself that power had gone out of Him"—and you will feel the same thing; there are people who spiritually and morally have to suck the vitals out of you, and if you don't keep up the supply from the life of Jesus Christ, you will be like an exhausted volcano before long. You must keep that up and let them nourish themselves from you until they are able to stand on their own feet and take direct life from Him.

The throes of the ultimate! Carlyle said of Tennyson: "Alfred is always carrying about chaos with him and turning it into cosmos." It is a good thing to be chaotic; it means there is a terrific possibility of development. The same thing spiritually, there is chaos in our lives that God is turning into the right cosmos; in the meantime, *look unto Jesus* and take the next step as it comes. If it is unrelieved rigors, get through the thing and you will be a tremendous assistance to men who are going through the same thing. It is not for you to lambast them for not being where you are, but for you to see to it that you are good nourishing stuff for them in God's hands.

Y.M.C.A. Hut, 12 August 1917

VOICE AND VISION

"Let the redeemed of the LORD say so" (Ps. 107:2).

We are apt to use words without having any idea of their meaning. In a crisis a word is really an "open sesame," and in certain spiritual, moral, and emotional crises if we do not say the word, emancipation will never be ours. Think of it in a simple way. When a child knows it has done something wrong and you want him to say he is sorry, the natural inclination of the child is stubbornly to refuse to say he *is* sorry; but until he does say so, there is no emancipation for him on to a higher level in his own life. This is the key to the way we are built all through; it is true not only in a child's life but in the moral domain, and emphatically true in the spiritual domain. Many of us are on the verge of a spiritual vision the realization of which never becomes ours because we will not open our mouths to "say so." We have to "say so" before we "feel so." The writer to the Hebrews speaks of the "sacrifice of praise." If we only praise when we feel like praising, it is simply an undisciplined expression, but if we deliberately go over the neck of our disinclination and offer the sacrifice of praise, we are emancipated by our very statements. We can slay a grousing mood by stating what we believe, and we are emancipated into a higher level of life immediately; but the "say so" must come before the emancipation is ours.

213

The Reserve That Ruins Spirituality

". . . with the mouth confession is made to salvation" (Rom. 10:10).

That is, to the realization of the salvation for which we believe. In the Bible confession and testimony are put in a prominent place, and the test of a man's moral caliber is the "say so." I may try and make myself believe a hundred and one things, but they will never be mine until I "say so." "With the heart one believes . . . ." "Heart" means all that is meant by "me." If I say with my self what I believe and confess it with my mouth, I am lifted into the domain of that thing. This is always the price of spiritual emancipation. If a child is to be taken out of his sulky mood he has to go across the disinclination of his reserve and *say* something; and this is true of all moral and spiritual life. If I will not confess with my mouth what I believe in my heart, that particular phase of believing will never be mine actually. Assurance of faith is never gained by reserve but only by abandonment. In the matter of human love it is a great emancipation to have it expressed; there may be intuitions of the love, but the realization of it is not ours until it is expressed. Morally and spiritually we live, as it were, in sections, and the door from one section to another is by means of words, and until we say the right word the door will not open. The right word is always based on the killing of the disinclination which belongs to a lower section.

Reserve is an unmitigated curse, not the reserve which indicates that there is power behind, but the reserve that refuses to go over the neck of its own pride. "If I confess this thing I shall have to forgo my reserve and take a further step on." That is the reserve that ruins spirituality. Emancipation comes through the "say so"; when we confess, the door opens, and life rushes on to a higher platform.

The Realization That Really Speaks

"When you pray, say, 'Our Father . . .'" (Luke 11:2).

"But I don't feel that God is my Father." Jesus said to say it—"say, 'Our Father,'" and you will suddenly discover that He is. The safeguard against moral imprisonment is prayer. Don't pray according to your moods, but resolutely launch out on God; say "Our Father," and before you know where you are, you are in a larger room. The door into a moral or spiritual emancipation which you wish to enter is a word. As soon as you are prepared to abandon your reserve and say the word, the door opens and in rushes the Godward side of things and you are lifted on to another platform immediately. "Speech makes a full man." If you want to encourage your own life in spiritual things, talk about them. Beware of the reserve that keeps to itself, that wants to develop spirituality alone; spirituality must be developed in the open. Shyness is often unmitigated conceit, an unconscious overestimation of your own worth; you are not prepared to speak until you have a proper audience. If you talk in the wrong mood, you will remain in the wrong mood and put the illegitimate on the throne; but if you talk in the mood which comes from revelation, emancipation will be yours. A preacher has no business to stir up emotions without giving his hearers some issue of will on which to transact.

The Revelation That Rightly Sees

"Go, stand in the temple and speak to the people all the words of this life" (Acts 5:20).

A man may betray Jesus Christ by speaking too many words, and he may betray Him through keeping his mouth shut. The revelation that perceives is that which recklessly states what it believes. When you stand up before your fellow-men and confess something about Jesus Christ, you feel you have no one to support you in the matter, but as you testify you begin to find the reality of your spiritual possessions, and there rushes into you the realization of a totally new life. "Be still, and know that I am God." When a man is able to state that he believes in God, it reacts on all his relationships. The thing that preserves a man from panic is his relationship to God; if he is only related to himself and to his own courage, there may come a moment when his courage gives out.

Some of us are living on too low a level, and remember, the door is shut on our side, not on God's. As soon as we will "say so," the door opens and the salvation for which we believe is ours in actual possession. Things only become clear as we say them. Too often we are like the child who will not do anything but murmur. We grouse and refuse to say the emancipating word which is within our reach all the time. As soon as we say the emancipating word, we undo the door and there rushes into us a higher and better life, and the revelation becomes real. "I must get out of this cabined, confined place"—then say the right word. If you have not received, ask; if you have not found, seek; if the door is shut, knock. When you are up against barriers, the way out is to "say so," then you will be emancipated, and your "say so" will not only be an emancipation for yourself, but someone else will enter into the light. We have to get rid of the reserve which keeps us starved and away from our fellowmen, that keeps us from getting what we should have. We have no business to live a driveling kind of life with barely sufficient for our own needs, we ought to enter into the storehouse and come out with riches for ourselves and ample to hand on to others. There are some people we are always the better for meeting; they do not talk piously, but somehow they give us a feeling of emancipation, they have a larger horizon. The reason is that they have opened the door for themselves by their "say so," and now the Word of God becomes spirit and life through them to others.

THE PLANE OF SPIRITUAL VIGOR

"Therefore, since Christ suffered for us in the flesh, arm yourselves also with the same mind, for he who has suffered in the flesh has ceased from sin" (1 Pet. 4:1).

Peter is dealing with the dangers that beset the spiritual man, dangers of which the average man is unaware. As long as a man sets out to be merely healthy-minded, the further he keeps away from Jesus Christ the better. The spiritual man must deliberately enter into the zone where he suffers in the flesh. If I am to be identified with Jesus Christ in this life, I must lay my account with the fact that I am going to be troubled in the flesh in a way I would not be if I were not so related to Him, because the last stake of the enemy is in the flesh.

The Discipline in the Flesh

"Therefore, since Christ suffered . . . in the flesh."

Suffering

How did Jesus Christ suffer in the flesh? Not because He was diseased or because He was more delicately strung than we are, but because He was differently related to God, He suffered "according to the will of God," that is, He let almighty

God do His whole will in and through Him without asking His permission; He did not live His life in the flesh from the point of view of realizing Himself. Any number of us suffer in the flesh who have not ceased from sin, but Peter's meaning is, "he who has suffered in the flesh [as Christ suffered in the flesh] has ceased from sin."

God will not shield us from the requirements of saints. When once we are related to life as Jesus was on the basis of redemption, He expects us to be to other people what He has been to us, and that will mean suffering in the flesh because it entails losing the aim of self-realization and basing everything on Christ realization, and as soon as we do that, other people will wipe their feet on us. No man is designed by nature to take the wiping of other people's feet, he can only do it when he can say with the apostle Paul, "I know how to be abased." Beware of the line of thinking which has sympathy with your sufferings but has no sympathy with Jesus Christ. Arm yourself with the mind of Christ, and the very suffering you go through will benefit others.

The Discipline in the Mind

"Arm yourselves also with the same mind."

Strenuousness

Some people have on an armor of innocence, like Tennyson's knight, whose "strength was as the strength of ten because his heart was pure"; others have on an armor of love. Paul says, "Put on the whole armor of God." Don't rely on anything less than that, clothe yourself with your relationship to God, maintain it. If you do not arm yourself with the armor of God, you are open to interferences in your hidden personal life from supernatural powers which you cannot control; but buckle on the armor, bring yourself into real living contact with God, and you are garrisoned not only in the conscious realm but in the depths of your personality beneath the conscious realm. "Praying always," says Paul. Every time we pray our horizon is altered, our attitude to things is altered, not sometimes but every time, and the amazing thing is that we don't pray more. Prayer is a complete emancipation, it keeps us on the spiritual plane. When you are at one with another mind there is a telepathic influence all the time, and when born from above the communion is between God and yourself; keep that going, says Peter. "Arm yourselves also with the same mind."

Are you neglecting prayer? No matter what else is neglected, switch back at once; if you don't you will be a dangerous influence to the people round about you. Watch the snare of self-pity—"Why should I go through this?" Be careful, you are a danger spot. I feel as if Jesus Christ were staggered with surprise at some of us, amazed at the things we say to Him, astonished at our attitude to Him, at the sulks we get into, because we have forgotten to arm ourselves with the same mind.

The Discipline in the Experience

"For he who has suffered in the flesh has ceased from sin."

Sanctification

The characteristic of the life now that you have ceased from sin is that you no longer do the things you used to do. "For we have spent enough of our past lifetime in doing the will of the Gentiles . . . . In regard to these, they think it strange that you do not run with them in the same flood of dissipation, speaking evil of you" (1 Pet. 4:3–4). "Let all that finish for you," says Peter, "stand now on a new basis, on the plane of the spiritual. See that you remain in identification with the sufferings of Jesus, and fill up that which is lacking of the afflictions of Christ." That is the plane of spiritual vigor.

How am I going to maintain my relationship to God on the spiritual plane, and keep the broad horizon that will help other men? "He who believes in Me," says Jesus, "out of his heart will flow rivers of living water." The radiating influence from one person rightly related to God is incalculable; he may not say much, but you feel different, the pressure has gone, you are in contact with one who is on a different plane.

Arm yourselves with the mind of Christ, maintain your life on the plane of spiritual vigor, and you will find that other people will suck nourishment and sustenance for their life out of you. Virtue will go out of you, and if you do not remain true to Jesus, you will collapse; there must be the continual supply, the continual drawing on the unsearchable riches of Jesus.

THE SENSE OF AWE

The Dread Face of His Detachment

"And as they followed they were afraid" (Mark 10:32).

The disciples had been living in closest intimacy with Jesus, but now they begin to see that there is a dread side to His life. He has an attitude to things which is not easy to understand, and it fills them with fear. There are different kinds of fear. We know what fear is in the physical domain, and in the moral domain; but in the spiritual domain a man's fear is not for his own skin at all, but, as it were, fear that his hero won't get through. This was the disciples' fear; it seemed as if all they had expected Jesus to do would end in nothing. Not one of them knew what Jesus was after, but still they followed, and they were afraid. Many of us are supernaturally solemn about our religion because it is not real. As soon as our religion becomes real, it is possible to have humor in connection with it. There are occasions, nevertheless, when there is not only no humor, but when humor is unfit; there is a dread sense of detachment from our ordinary attitude to things which fills us with awe. We are all apt to interpret Jesus from our own standpoint; we get too familiar with Him, and a moral surgery of events is necessary before we can understand His standpoint. We get a glimpse of what Jesus is after, and

His attitude makes it look as if He were absolutely insensitive to our aims; or else He has a point of view of which we know nothing and the sense of detachment continually comes. Jesus is treating us as He treated Martha and Mary; because He loved them He stayed two days where He was and did not come in answer to their prayer. Jesus Christ can afford to be misunderstood; we cannot. Our weakness lies in always wanting to vindicate ourselves. Jesus never takes the trouble to alter mistakes; He knows they will alter themselves.

All through our Lord's life this note continually recurs, "Behold, we are going up to Jerusalem"; yet He was not in a panic to get there. He set His face like a flint to go to Jerusalem, the place where He was to reach the climax of His Father's will. There was no misunderstanding as to what it would mean when He got there, namely, death, with a peculiar significance. Whenever Jesus talked to His disciples about His cross, they misunderstood Him; until at last they began to see a deeper depth than they had ever thought, a relation to things in His life about which they knew nothing. They did not know what Jesus was heading for, and as they followed they were afraid.

It is a most humiliating thing to find that we have estimated the man with whom we are familiar on too low a level; to discover that after all he has a bigger relation to things than we have ever had. If we are going to estimate another man's point of view (which is as valuable as our own), we must take the trouble to find out the kind of man he is behind his words. When we take Jesus Christ's words about His cross, the least thing we can do is to endeavor to get at His mind behind His words. Jesus says things from a different point of view from ours, and unless we receive His Spirit, we do not even begin to see what He is driving at. "He . . . said to them, 'Receive the

Holy Spirit'" (John 20:22). ". . . the Helper, the Holy Spirit . . . He will teach you all things . . . "(John 14:26).

The Disciplining Force of His Delays

"I still have many things to say to you, but you cannot bear them now" (John 16:12).

"Why can I not follow You now?" asked Peter. "You can-not follow Me now," said Jesus, "but you shall follow Me afterward." The delays of Jesus discipline us while they con-tinually tantalize us. "If You are the Christ, tell us plainly." Jesus answered them, "I told you, and you do not believe"; they were not in the place where they could understand. Un-derstanding comes only by obedience, never by intellect. Our Lord does not hide things from us, but they are unbearable until we get into a fit condition of life on the inside. "Why does not God tell us these things?" we say. He is telling us all the time, but we are unable to perceive His meaning. The force of the disciplining delays lies in the fact that God is engineer-ing our circumstances in order to bring us into a fit moral state to understand. "Before I was afflicted I went astray, but now I keep Your word." The delay in interpretation depends on our willingness to obey. Obedience is always the secret of under-standing. For instance, if there is the tiniest grudge in our spirit against another, from that second, spiritual penetration into the knowledge of God will cease. "Therefore if you bring your gift to the altar, and there remember that your brother has something against you, leave your gift there before the altar," says Jesus, "and go your way. First be reconciled to your brother, and then come and offer your gift."

It is a great emancipation in a man's life when he learns that spiritual and moral truths can only be gained by obe-dience, never by intellectual curiosity. All God's revelations are sealed, and they will never be opened by philosophy, or by thinking; whereas the tiniest fragment of obedience will bring a man right through into the secret of God's attitude to things. Mere intellectual training turns a man into a psychological ostrich; his head is all right, but in actual life he is left floundering. How are we going to make plain the things which are obscure to us just now? Intellectual curiosity will not take us one inch inside moral problems, but as soon as we obey, in the tiniest matter, instantly we see.

The Dawning Fear of His Deity

"And when I saw Him, I fell at His feet as dead" (Rev. 1:17).

These words were uttered by the disciple who knew Jesus most intimately, the one who laid his head on Jesus' bosom, the disciple "whom Jesus loved"—when He saw Him in His unveiled deity, he fell at His feet as one dead, paralyzed with amazement; then there came the voice he had learned to know in the days of His flesh, saying, "Do not be afraid; I am the First and the Last."

Has our discipleship to Jesus a sense of awe about it, or do we patronize Him? At the beginning we were sure that we knew all about Jesus, but now we are not quite so sure; He is taken up with a point of view we know nothing about, and we can no longer be familiar with Him. Instead of walking to triumph as the disciples expected Jesus to do, He goes to disaster; instead of bringing peace, He brings a sword. In every way Jesus enters into "somewhere" that fills us with awe. A time comes when He is no longer counselor and comrade. With one stride He goes deliberately in front and says, "Follow Me," and the things that lie ahead are wildly terrible to us. There is nothing familiar now about Jesus, and there is a dread sense of detachment.

It may be that in our inner life Jesus is teaching us by the disciplining force of His delays. "I expected God to answer my prayer, but He has not." He is bringing us to the place where by obedience we shall see what it is He is after. It may be that, like John, we know Jesus intimately, then suddenly He appears with no familiar characteristic at all, and the only thing we can do is to fall at His feet as one dead. There are times when God cannot reveal Himself in any other way than in His majesty. And out of the midst of the terror there comes the voice we know, saying to us personally, "Do not be afraid." When once His touch comes like that, nothing can at all cast us into fear again.

SPIRITUAL MALINGERING

"O foolish ones, and slow of heart to believe . . ." (Luke 24:25).

To believe is literally to commit. Belief is a moral act, and Jesus makes an enormous demand of a man when He asks him to believe in Him. To be "a believer in Jesus" means to bank our confidence in Him, to stake our soul upon His honor—"I know whom I have believed . . . ." We pray, "Lord, increase our faith," and we try to pump up faith, but it does not come. What is wrong? The moral surrender to Jesus has not taken place. Will I surrender to Jesus from the real center of my life, and deliberately and willfully stake my confidence in what He says? Many of us use religious jargon; we talk about believing in God, but our actual life proves that we do not really believe one tenth of what we profess.

If you can solve your problems without Jesus, then solve them, but don't blink any of the facts. "Let not your heart be troubled," says Jesus. Does Jesus really mean that He wants us to be untroubled in heart? "Believe also in Me"—that is, make room for Me, especially in the matters where you cannot go. As we bring the child mind to what Jesus says about things, we will begin to manifest the miracle of an undisturbed heart. In the cross our Lord deals with everything that keeps a man's heart disturbed.

Unrealized Forgiveness

"... preach ... the unsearchable riches of Christ" (Eph. 3:8).

"The unsearchable riches of Christ"—yet we often live as if our heavenly Father had cut us off with nothing! We think it is a sign of real modesty to say at the end of a day, "Oh well, I have just got through, but it has been a severe tussle." We carry our religion as if it were a headache; there is neither joy nor power nor inspiration in it, none of the grandeur of the unsearchable riches of Christ about it, none of the passion of hilarious confidence in God. And the word of our Lord comes home to us that we are half-imbecile children with regard to the things of God; in effect, "When will you believe what I say?" Instead of our life being a recommendation of Christianity it is apt to make others say, "Is that what you call Christianity? Why, I have a good deal more moral life than there is in that kind of anemic whine!" There is nothing in it of the robust strength of confidence in God which will go through anything, and stake its all on the honor of Jesus Christ. Christianity is the vital realization of the unsearchable riches of Christ.

"In Him we have redemption through His blood, the forgiveness of sins . . ." (Eph. 1:7). Brood on that statement. Divine forgiveness is part of the unsearchable riches that our ours through the redemption, and it is because we do not realize the miracle of God's forgiveness that spiritual malingering results, that is, we remain feeble and weak in Christian faith in order to evade the enormous demands that our faith makes on us. We talk glibly about forgiving when we have never been injured; when we are injured we know that it is not possible, apart from God's grace, for one human being to forgive another. "I will say no more about it, but I do not intend to forget what you have done." The forgiveness of God is altogether different. When God forgives, He never casts up at us the mean, miserable things we have done. "I have blotted out, like a thick cloud, your transgressions, and like a cloud, your sins." A cloud cannot be seen when it is gone.

"But that man will take advantage of God's forgiveness." Will I take advantage of God's forgiveness? No one on earth is more mean than I am, no one more capable of doing wrong, and yet we are always more afraid of the other fellow than of ourselves. The forgiveness of God means that we are forgiven into a new relationship, namely, into identification with God in Christ, so that the forgiven man is the holy man. The only explanation of the forgiveness of God and of the unfathomable depth of His forgetting is the blood of Jesus. We trample the blood of the Son of God under foot if we think we are forgiven in any other way. Forgiveness is the divine miracle of grace.

Unexplored Prayer Zone

"Having boldness to enter the Holiest by the blood of Jesus" (Heb. 10:19).

We are apt to think of prayer as an aesthetic religious exercise. The revelation made here is that we have freedom to go straight to the heart of God, as simply as a child going to his mother, by "a new and living way which He consecrated for us." Our approach is due entirely to the vicarious identification of our Lord with sin. It is not our earnestness that brings us into touch with God, not our stated times of prayer, but the vitalizing death of our Lord Jesus Christ.

Unselfish Sanctification

"Therefore Jesus also, that He might sanctify the people with His own blood . . ." (Heb. 13:12).

"For their sakes I sanctify Myself." Jesus separated His holy self to the will of His Father. The one characteristic of our Lord's human life was His submission to His Father. "The Son can do nothing of Himself." Our Lord did not come to do His own will. And we are not made holy for ourselves. Sanctification means being identified with Jesus until all the springs of our being are in Him. ". . . that they may be one just as We are one." We do not experience sanctification for any purpose other than God's purpose.

Forgiveness of sins is the gift of God; entrance into the holiest is the gift of God; sanctification is the gift of God. A man cannot save his own soul, or forgive his sins, or get hold of God in prayer, or sanctify himself; but Jesus reveals that God has done all this in redemption—are we going to bank on what He has done? As we do, new forces will come into our experiential life drawn entirely from the unsearchable riches, ours through the redemption. Christian faith means putting our confidence in the efficacy of Christ's work.

When God says we have "redemption through His blood," are we going to commit ourselves to Him and bank on His word? When God says we have "boldness to enter the Holiest by the blood of Jesus," are we going to draw near in faith? There is boundless entrance into the holiest by the way He has consecrated for us. When God says, "Jesus also, that He might sanctify the people with His own blood . . ." are we going to believe Him? By sanctification we understand experientially what Paul says in 1 Corinthians 1:30—"But of Him you are in Christ Jesus, who became for us . . . sanctification." Sanctification is an impartation, a gift, not an imitation. Sanctification means, "Christ . . . formed in you." Jesus gives us the life inherent in Himself.

"When the Son of Man comes, will He really find faith on the earth?"—the faith that banks on Him in spite of all the confusion? Or will we have to say, "No, Lord, I never trusted You for one moment; I used religious jargon, I put on a religious plaster when I was sore, but I had no confidence whatever in anything You said." We have made Christianity to mean the saving of our skins. Christianity means staking ourselves on the honor of Jesus; His honor means that He will see us through time, death, and eternity. Do we credit Jesus Christ with knowing what He is talking about, or are we half imbecile with regard to these truths?

When we are standing face to face with Jesus, and He says, "Do you believe this?" our faith is as natural as breathing, and we say "Yes Lord," and are staggered and amazed that we were so stupid as not to trust Him before.

THE DEEP EMBARRASSMENTS OF GOD

Hosea 11

When a man who has known God turns away from Him, it is God who brings out his embarrassments and engineers his enemies. There are barriers placed by God, entanglements of embarrassment, by means of which God says to the personal spirit of the man, in effect, "Not that way, My son; if you go that way, you will break your neck and be ruined." It is impossible for a man to go wrong easily; he may drift a tremendously long way easily, he may come to have different standards easily; but if a man has known better than he does now, he has not arrived there easily. "The way of the unfaithful is hard" (Pro. 13:15).

The Mothering Affection of God (Hos. 11:1–4)

"When Israel was a child, I loved him . . ." (Hos. 11:1).

The mothering affection of God is revealed all through the Old Testament. A man won't talk of it because it is too precious. "I have nourished and brought up children" (Isa. 1:2). "As one whom his mother comforts, so I will comfort you" (Isa. 66:13). "I remember you, the kindness of your youth"

(Jer. 2:2). When a man is born again of the Spirit of God, he does not walk by faith, but by sight; everything thrills, it is a delight to be spiritual.

We have all felt the mothering affection of God; are we departing from what we saw then? "My people are bent on backsliding from Me." Backsliding is turning away from what we know to be best to what we know is second-best. If you have known God better than you know Him today and are deliberately settling down to something less than the best—watch, for you will not escape; God will bring embarrassments out against you, in your private life, in your domestic life; He will enmesh you on the right hand and on the left. Compare your life with the life of one who has never known God—"they are not in trouble as other men; nor are they plagued like other men."

The Maturity of Attainment (Hos. 11:5–7)

"My people are bent on backsliding from Me . . ." (Hos. 11:7).

Never estimate a man under thirty as you would estimate him when over forty. The vices of a man who has not reached maturity are nearly always worse than he really is and his virtues better than he really is. After maturity is reached, no vice or virtue is an accident, it is a dead set of attainment. The same is true spiritually. For a while God seems to overlook the blunders and wrongdoing of His children—"Truly, these times of ignorance God overlooked, but now commands all men everywhere to repent" (Acts 17:30); but when they come to maturity He makes no allowance. Spiritual maturity is not reached by the passing of the years, but by obedience. When Solomon attained to maturity, this significant thing was said of him, that his heart was turned away after other gods; God brought out his embarrassments and engineered his enemies and the things that brought him confusion and distress.

It is easy to have the attitudes of religion, but it is the temper of our mind we have to watch. It is not the wrong things, but our temper of mind in serving God that will turn us from Him. A man may have preached to others and have attained, but now the secret defects of his devotion have come to light; his heart is turned away from God. If we only believe in Jesus because He delivers us from hell, we will forsake Him in two seconds if He crosses our purposes or goes contrary to our personal disposition of mind.

It is the motive in doing right things that may be wrong. Doing a wrong thing may be a haphazard affair to a large extent, but a wrong temper of mind is never a haphazard affair. It is a determined enthronement of something other than God. A man may look all right in his ostensible religious life, he may have had a vivid religious history, but his private life may be rotten. It is a terrible thing to become blunt and insensitive. Sin destroys the power of knowing that we sin, and one of the dangerous outcomes of a mood that is not right with God is that it turns a man into a prig.

The Mastering of Antagonism

". . . the LORD . . . will roar like a lion . . ." (Hos. 11:10).

It will be a question of slaughter, upset, and disaster, then, says God, "they shall follow Me again." If a man has reached maturity and has deliberately put something other than God before him, and is not walking humbly with God, then God will bring things out against him, his enemies will be organized by God. God brought out against His own people nations that did not know Him. Others seem to do wrong and escape, but God is gathering you round, He comes up against you on the right hand and on the left. If you have known Me, says Jesus, and pretend to be abiding in Me and yet are not bringing forth fruit, either My Father will remove you, or if you persist in masquerading, men will gather you and burn you in the fire. The exposing of hypocrisy is never a shock to the cause of God. Judgment begins at the house of God. No man is ever a stumbling block in the way of another who does the thing he ought to do.

"While you have the light, believe in the light." Believe what you see in your best mood and not what you see in a dark mood. Watch the temper of your mind. Why do you pray? Why are you religious? Because of a consuming passion for a particular set of your beliefs to be enthroned and proved right, or because of a consuming passion for Jesus Christ? If you are religious, beware lest you are keener on the plan of salvation than on the Savior.

GETTING INTO GOD'S STRIDE

"Enoch walked with God" (Gen. 5:24).

The test of a man's religious life and character is not what he does in the exceptional moments of his life, but what he does in the ordinary times when he is not before the spotlight, when there is nothing tremendous or exciting on. John looked upon Jesus "coming toward him, and said, 'Behold! The Lamb of God!'" In learning to walk with God there is the difficulty of getting into His stride; when we have got into His stride, what manifests itself in the life is the characteristic of God. The idea in the Bible is not only that we might be saved, but that we might become sons and daughters of God, and that means having the attitude of God to things.

Individual Discouragement and Personal Enlargement (Ex. 2:11–14)

"Now it came to pass in those days, when Moses was grown, that he went out to his brethren and looked at their burdens" (Ex. 2:11).

Moses was learned in all the wisdom of the Egyptians, he was a mighty man and a great statesman, and when he saw the oppression of his people he felt that God had called him out to deliver them, and in the righteous indignation of his own spirit he started to right their wrongs. God is never in a hurry. After the first big strike for God and for the right thing, God allowed Moses, the only man who could deliver his own people, to be driven into the desert to feed sheep—forty years of blank discouragement. Then when God appeared and told him to go and bring forth the people, Moses said, "Who am I that I should go?" The big "I am" had gone, and the little "I am" had taken its place. At first, Moses was certain he was the man, and so he was, but he was not fit yet. He set out to deliver the people in a way that had nothing of the stride of God about it. Moses was right in the individual aspect, but he was not the man for the work until he had learned communion with God, and it took forty years in the desert while God worked through him in ways of terrific personal enlargement before he recognized this.

We may have the vision of God, a very clear understanding of what God wants—wrongs to be righted, the salvation of sinners, and the sanctification of believers; we are certain we see the way out, and we start to do the thing. Then comes something equivalent to the forty years in the wilderness, discouragement, disaster, upset, as if God had ignored the whole thing. When we are thoroughly flattened out, God comes back and revives the call, and we get the quaver in, and say, "Oh, who am I, that I should go?" We have to learn the first great stride of God—"I AM WHO I AM . . . has sent . . . you." We have to learn that our individual effort for God is an impertinence; our individuality must be rendered incandescent by a personal relationship to God, and that is not learned easily. The individual man is lost in his personal union with God, and what is manifested is the stride and the power of God. "I indeed baptize you with water unto repentance, but He who is coming after me is mightier than I, whose sandals I

237

am not worthy to carry. He will baptize you with the Holy Spirit and fire" (Matt. 3:11).

Moses had to learn this, and our Lord taught His disciples the same thing, "You did not choose Me, but I chose you and appointed you that you should go and bear fruit, and that your fruit should remain, that whatever you ask the Father in My name He may give you" (John 15:16), and He emphasizes it in John 17—"that they may be one just as We are one."

How many of us have gone through this experience of getting into the stride of God? We have the vision, the real life is there, but we have not got into God's stride about the work and we fix on the individual aspect, "This is what God wants me to do." That is only my individual interpretation of what God wants me to do. Our efforts spring from the certainty that we understand God, and in our prayers we dictate to God what we think He ought to do. The individuality suffers terrible discouragement until we learn to get into personal union with God, then we experience an extraordinary enlargement. When the Spirit of God gets me into stride with God, He sheds abroad the love of God in my heart—"God so loved the world . . ." (John 3:16). I have my personal life, my home life, my national life, my individual attitude to things, and it takes time for me to believe that the Almighty pays no regard to any of these; I come slowly into the idea that God ignores my prejudices, wipes them out absolutely.

Inspired Direction and Personal Expression (Ezek. 3:12–17)

> "So the Spirit lifted me up and took me away, and I went in bitterness, in the heat of my spirit; but the hand of the LORD was strong upon me" (Ezek. 3:14).

Ezekiel was inspired of God, God's message was blazing in him—"Wait till I get to the people, I'll tell them what God has said." But when he did get there, he sat down flabbergasted and was dumb for seven days, all his message gone from him; he hadn't the heart to say a solitary word. He was inspired surely enough, directed by God, the blazing message of God was in his heart; but when he saw the condition of his fellow exiles, all he could do was to sit down among them in their circumstances and let their circumstances talk to him. Ezekiel had his message, but he had not the communion of God's personal attitude expressed in the particular circumstances, and he sat dumbfounded for seven days. Then his attitude was, Have I still to give Your message? And God said, in effect, "Yes, now you can give it free from individual spleen in a way which gives exactly My interpretation." Ezekiel had the same message, but when he had come to the inspired direction of God he understood things differently.

We have a blazing inspiration from God, we see perfectly well that certain things are wrong, and we know that God will not minimize wrong, but we do not yet understand how to deal rightly with these things. We have our inspired direction, we know that God says men are to be delivered, but we have to remember that when we sit down as Ezekiel did where people are, there is a danger lest we lose all moral distinctions and powers of judging. The danger is that we are so completely overcome with pain over the result of sin in men's lives that we forget to deliver God's message. God says, in effect, "Remember, I am a holy God, and when you have come into right relationship with Me, then give My message." When Jesus said to the scribes and Pharisees, "How can you escape the condemnation of hell?" He was speaking not out of personal vindictiveness but with a background of the inevitable; He had exhibited God before them, yet they turned from Him and despised Him. These words were uttered by the being who died on Calvary, and must be read in the light of the cross.

Inscrutable Disaster and Personal Experience

"And he was three days without sight, and neither ate nor drank" (Acts 9:9).

Saul of Tarsus was "knocked out," and it took him three days to get his breath before he could begin to get into the stride of God. Who was Saul of Tarsus? A Pharisee of the Pharisees, a man of superb integrity and conscientiousness. If there ever was a conscientious objector it was Saul—"Indeed, I myself thought I must do many things contrary to the name of Jesus of Nazareth." He was conscientious when he hounded the followers of Jesus Christ to death. Then came disaster, all his world was flung to pieces. God arrested him, "He was three days without sight, and neither ate nor drank"; but out of the inscrutable disaster and upset God brought him into a personal experience of Himself. "But when it pleased God, who separated me from my mother's womb and called me through His grace, to reveal His Son in me, that I might preach Him among the Gentiles, I did not immediately confer with flesh and blood" (Gal. 1:15–16). For three years Saul went round about Sinai while the Holy Spirit blazed into him the things that became his epistles.

It is a painful business getting through into the stride of God; it means getting our "second wind" morally and spiritually. When I start walking with God, I have not taken three strides before I find He has outstripped me; He has different ways of doing things and I have to be trained and disciplined into His ways. It was said of Jesus, "He will not fail nor be discouraged," because He never worked from His own individual standpoint, but always from the standpoint of His Father.

Discouragement is "disenchanted egotism." We learn spiritual truth by atmosphere not by intellectual reasoning; God's spirit alters the atmosphere of our ways of looking at things, and things begin to be possible which never were possible before.

If you are going through a period of discouragement there is a big personal enlargement ahead. We have the stride of divine healing, of sanctification, of the second coming; all these are right, but the stride of God is never anything less than union with Himself.

Notes of the last sermon preached at Zeitoun, 4 October 1917

DISABLING SHADOWS ON THE SOUL

"Also when they are afraid of height, and of terrors in the way; when the almond tree blossoms, the grasshopper is a burden, and desire fails. For man goes to his eternal home, and the mourners go about the streets" (Eccl. 12:5).

Solomon is describing the last lap of a man's life when his nerves give way, and little things become an intolerable bur- den. There are things like this that come across us naturally and we have difficulty in tracing where they come from; they make us irritable or melancholy. Times when a fly or a mos- quito is more annoying than the devil himself. And the same thing is true spiritually; there are times when little things pes- ter and annoy and there is nothing in us big enough to cope with them. This verse is a picture of the shadows which come across a man's soul not because he has done wrong or has backslidden; there is nothing definite about it, but he finds himself belittling everything; there is no vision or power or grandeur in anything. Nothing has been done wrong, there is no reason why you should feel your feet like lead and your heart like ice, and yet you seem about three inches high, with the mind of an insect, irritated and annoyed over everything there is. "What is the good of anything at all? What is the good of having done my duty? of praying, or believing in God?" That aspect of things comes over and over again in the Bible and in our own experience. It happens out here physically; you suddenly feel "knocked out" and you don't know why you should. It is a symbol for what happens spiritually.

The Weariness of the Way

"And let us not grow weary while doing good, for in due season we shall reap if we do not lose heart" (Gal. 6:9).

When a man sins magnificently he is always punished monotonously, that is the ingenuity of punishment (as with Samson). We know about the weariness that comes from wrong-doing, but Paul says, "Do not grow weary while doing good." We all experience the weariness that comes from wrong-doing, but I want to mention the weariness which annoys us because we don't know how it came, why our life suddenly lost all its interest. The point to note is that weariness does come in well-doing, when everything becomes listless. It has no business to be though; it is a sickness of the soul. What is the cure? The cure is that of a right vision. Every man has the power to slay his own weariness, not by "bucking up" as you do physically, but by suddenly looking at things from a different standpoint. "Why are you cast down, O my soul? And why are you disquieted within me? Hope in God; for I shall yet praise Him, the help of my countenance and my God" (Ps. 43:5). It is a tremendous thing to know that God reigns and rules and rejoices, and that His joy is our strength. The confidence of a Christian is that God is never in the sulks. ". . . the Father of lights, with whom there is no variation or shadow of turning."

The Wasting in the Way

"Nor of the pestilence that walks in darkness, nor of the destruction that lays waste at noonday" (Ps. 91:6).

In our modern Christian vocabulary we have lost sight of a sin the monks used to recognize—the sin of "Accidie." It took hold of a man at noon and he suddenly became vilely irritable. It is the inarticulate things which are the most devastating of all. Dante places in the deepest cycle of hell the people who were guilty of the sin of gloom. This wasting in the way shows itself in irritability, bad temper, and melancholy; you don't seem able to "buck yourself up." If you sit down when you are in the dumps, you are a plague spot to all around you.

The Wandering from Worship

"If you turn away your foot from the Sabbath, from doing your pleasure on My holy day, and call the Sabbath a delight . . ." (Isa. 58:13).

If I have known God and have seen Him in my clear moments, and in any moment of sluggishness have turned away from Him, instantly weariness comes. In spiritual life the danger is to make the effect the cause. As soon as I make doing right my aim, I get weary. This is the right attitude: "For we do not preach ourselves, but Christ Jesus the Lord, and ourselves your servants for Jesus' sake" (2 Cor. 4:5). When I get my eyes off Him I begin to get weary. I am kept from wasting in the way only as I abide under the shadow of the Almighty and stake my all in confidence in God. I have nothing to do with the results, but only with maintaining my relationship to Him.

"If you refrain from doing your pleasure on My holy day." In every family, and in every Christian community, keeping the Sabbath day holy is a chance for ostensibly declaring to the world that we recognize that God is the head.

Wandering from the vision you once had accounts for weariness and wasting. When you were in your best moments you saw things in a certain way. Believe what you saw then;

don't believe what you saw in the lower mood (see John 12:36). The best tonic you can have comes from the man or woman who is merciless to your weariness or wandering; to pander to weariness which has no definite cause is sinful. If you are sick or ill, that has to be handled in a different way; but if there is weariness or wasting and you cannot get at the cause of it, this is the reason—you have neglected private prayer, neglected worship, neglected doing something you know perfectly well you should have done. It hasn't yet come the length of sin; it is a defect no one notices, but sadness creeps on my soul whenever I deflect from the highest I know.

You have nothing to do with anyone else; look after the vision of your own life, and you will be a benediction to every one with whom you come in contact (John 7:38). Don't try to find out whether you are a blessing, pay attention to the source, then out of you will flow rivers of living water that you know nothing about. But if you cut yourself off from the source, and gloom away from God, your weariness and wasting is worse than an epidemic, it is a heavy disease to the spiritual community around.

Let me watch whether I am wandering from worship, from the highest I know; I do not wander alone. The wasting that destroys me in the noontide of my spiritual life, or the weariness that comes over me, is a thing that hinders others. Let me get back again to the place where the airs and the light and the liberty of God come, and all the time there flows through the inspiration to others.

Note to the Reader

The publisher invites you to share your response to the message of this book by writing Discovery House Publishers, P.O. Box 3566, Grand Rapids, MI 49501 U.S.A. or by calling 800-283-8333. For information about other Discovery House publications, contact us at the same address and phone number.

My Utmost for His Highest
by *Oswald Chambers*
    The classic devotional bestseller. These powerful words will
refresh those who need encouragement, brighten the way of those in
difficulty, and strengthen personal relationships with Christ. A book
to use every day for the rest of your life.
Audio Tape Edition: The complete work on twelve cassettes.

The Oswald Chambers Library
    Powerful insights on topics of interest to every believer:

The Shadow of an Agony/The Highest Good
    The mystery of suffering and Christian conduct.

Shade of His Hand
    A challenging look at Ecclesiastes.

Bringing Sons Into Glory/Making All Things New
    The glories of the great truths of salvation and redemption.

Baffled to Fight Better
    Job and the problem of suffering.

If You Will Ask
    Reflections on the power of prayer.

The Love of God
    An intimate look at the Father-heart of God.

Not Knowing Where
    Keen spiritual direction through knowing and trusting God.

The Place of Help
    Thoughts on daily needs of the Christian life.

Order from your favorite bookstore or from:

DISCOVERY HOUSE PUBLISHERS
Box 3566
Grand Rapids, MI 49501
Call toll-free: 1-800-283-8333